Happy Endings and Horror Stories
from Real-Life Relationships

Most Perigee Books are available at special quantity discounts for bulk purchases for sales promotions, premiums, fund-raising, or educational use. Special books, or book excerpts, can also be created to fit specific needs.

For details, write: Special Markets, The Berkley Publishing Group, 375 Hudson Street, New York, New York 10014.

You Know He's a Keeper

Happy Endings and Horror Stories
from Real-Life Relationships

You Know He's a Loser...

LINDA LEE SMALL *and*

NORINE DWORKIN

A Perigee Book

A Perigee Book
Published by The Berkley Publishing Group
A division of Penguin Group (USA) Inc.
375 Hudson Street
New York, New York 10014

Copyright © 2003 by Linda Lee Small and Norine Dworkin
Text design by Tiffany Estreicher
Cover design by Ben Gibson
Cover art by Marcos Chin

All rights reserved. This book, or parts thereof, may not be reproduced in any form without permission. The scanning, uploading, and distribution of this book via the Internet or via any other means without the permission of the publisher is illegal and punishable by law. Please purchase only authorized electronic editions, and do not participate in or encourage electronic piracy of copyrighted materials. Your support of the authors' rights is appreciated.

First edition: January 2004
www.penguin.com
This Library of Congress Cataloging in-Publication Data

You know he's a keeper, you know he's a loser : happy endings and horror stories from real-life relationships / [compiled by] Linda Lee Small and Norine Dworkin.—1st ed.
    p.cm
"A Perigee book."
ISBN 0-399-52886-5
    1. Man-woman relationships—Anecdotes. 2. Mate selection—Anecdotes. I. Small, Linda Lee. II. Dworkin, Norine.

HQ801.Y674 2004
306.7—dc22

2003062418

Printed in the United States of America

10 9 8 7 6 5 4 3 2 1

For the Keepers in our lives:
David Howard Krupnick (1942–1998)
and
Stewart Michael McDaniel

Acknowledgments

We are deeply indebted to all of the incredible women who shared their happy endings and horror stories with us. Without their generosity, humor, and candor this book would not have been possible. We'd also like to thank the members of the Park Slope Women's Writers Group, who enthusiastically read the first draft of our book proposal and eagerly contributed stories of their own.

Special thanks go to Mary Harmon who kindly sent many of her friends our way. And to Stephanie Bloom, Maria Bruno, Marty Munson, and Bernie Maciol who organized gals-only get-togethers to introduce us to more women than we could have ever met on our own. And to New Age Health Spa in Neversink, New York, which graciously provided us with even more opportunities to talk with women about the Keepers and Losers in their lives.

Many, many thanks also go to Kevin Haynes and Claudia Shaum who read early drafts of the manuscript and offered invaluable suggestions to make it better.

Finally, very special thanks go to our agent Agnes Birnbaum of Bleecker Street Associates who was an ardent advocate of our project and provided wonderful advice and support as we put this book together, and to our editor at Penguin Group, Michelle Howry, whose remarkable vision and dedication has made this book a Keeper.

INTRODUCTION

You Know He's a Keeper . . .

● LINDA LEE SMALL ●

Many years ago I was sharing a cab with Letty Cottin Pogrebin, the cofounder of *Ms.* magazine. It was Valentine's Day, and Letty wanted to know the most romantic thing my husband, David, had ever done to mark the occasion. She explained that she just loved Valentine's Day and "collected" romantic anecdotes. (What she ever did with them is for another book.) I couldn't recall a really special Valentine's Day because David wasn't a roses or sweep-you-off-your-feet kind of guy. But Letty persisted. "Okay then just tell me something romantic and wonderful he did." Ah, that was easier. So I told her the following story with the proviso that I didn't know how *romantic* it was:

> *I was away for the weekend covering a convention—ironically for* Ms. *magazine. I came back into the apartment late Sunday night just hours after David had left on his own business trip. I was tired, cranky, and hungry. On the refrigerator was a note:* "Dear Lovee"—*that's what David always called me*—"I bet you are tired, cranky and very hungry. Look inside." *When I opened the refrigerator, there was a plate of food waiting for me, complete with a mini bottle of wine already uncorked, slices of cheese, crackers, and a miniature vanilla cannoli. I ate my feast and smiled.*

After I finished telling the story, Letty paused for a second and said, "He's a Keeper."

I never thought about it in those terms. Until he died five years ago

David always let me know that he cherished me. And that's probably the best definition of a Keeper.

Shortly after David died, I had dinner with a younger friend, Norine Dworkin, who was in the middle of a divorce. We started sharing stories. I was trying to "introduce" her to David. Having just ended her five-year marriage, she had much different stories to share. "How," she wondered, "can you tell if the guy you are with is a Loser?" The more stories we shared, the more we decided that men send messages; it's just that women aren't always open to hearing them. That became the lightbulb moment for both of us. A book idea was born. . . .

INTRODUCTION

. . . You Know He's a Loser

NORINE DWORKIN

Over the next two years, as we put this book together, Linda talked with women about the men who brought sunshine and roses into their lives, and I interviewed gals about the toads they encountered. We approached women everywhere—bars, restaurants, bookstores, spas, the Internet, even a Greyhound bus. We polled our families and grilled our friends. Everyone we met we prodded, "Tell us your story."

To help me collect Loser stories, several girlfriends hosted gatherings where, fueled by *lots* of cocktails, women talked about the light-bulb moment when they knew the guy just had to go. The gals were often shy at first. But once they got rolling, the stories flowed, ever faster as they egged each other on. That's the thing. We've all been there. Some of us knew on the first date—or before there could even be a first date. For others, it took years for a relationship to unravel. But everyone's encountered at least one man who's done them wrong, and there's comfort and camraderie in sharing that experience.

Of course some stories were too cruel to be included, a reminder that there's a special Bad Guy category that goes beyond Loser. Instead we focused on the self-absorbed jerks, bald-faced liars, and mildly crazy dudes most of us run into. Some committed capital crimes of the heart, others only misdemeanors. Still others are just men who in different circumstances might even be Keepers.

Together these stories represent a community of women all riffing on the same themes. Hopefully they'll make you laugh, smile, sigh, groan, even wonder, *How could they?* And maybe think of your own relationship. One night my partner, Stewart, picked me up from a bar where I'd been listening to particularly depressing tales of no-good guys. He approached us cautiously, nervous that we'd turn on him in a man-hating frenzy.

"Oh no," I said, hugging him. "Hearing these tales makes me appreciate you *more*."

That's the thing about Losers. For all the aggravation and hurt they bring, having bumped into enough of them, when we do find our Keeper, we cherish him all the more.

You Know He's a Keeper

Happy Endings and Horror Stories
from Real-Life Relationships

You Know He's a Loser

I Give It a Thumbs Up

I thought my future husband, a lawyer, was a little insensitive when we first started going out. On one of our first dates he took me to see the rerelease of *Gone with the Wind*. At the end of part one, when Scarlett is down in the dirt swearing she will never go hungry again, I was crying. So was just about every other woman in the theater. Burt, however, was *laughing*. I mean out-loud laughing and shaking his head. Not a good sign, I thought.

But he really was attractive—6'3" and green eyed—and there was just something appealing about him. Shortly after, *I* picked the movie. It was *The Heart Is a Lonely Hunter* based on the novel by Carson McCullers. I don't even remember the entire plot, but it was a real gut-wrencher. At the end of the movie there was a lot of quiet sobbing—including me. I looked over at Burt, hoping he wasn't laughing again. There he was with tears streaming down his face. He reached over and took my hand. And I knew. That night he crawled into my heart.

It's been more than thirty years now. Anytime Burt thinks I'm annoyed with him or want him to be "nicer," he will often whisper to me, "The heart is a . . . " And that's all it takes to make me smile.

- Lee, Macon, Georgia

LOSER

Pop Goes the Weasel

A college friend introduced me to an aspiring actor at a small party. He seemed nice, so when he asked me out to the movies, I accepted. Movies are expensive in New York, and since I knew Mike wasn't always working, I was prepared to buy my own ticket. While waiting on line for snacks, he asked if I could also get the popcorn since he was a bit short. No problem. I had enough cash for a large popcorn—perfect to share.

Except we disagreed about the butter.

I refuse to put butter on my popcorn—movie popcorn has enough fat and calories as is. Mike wanted the butter. And he wasn't giving it up without a fight.

First he asked the kid behind the counter to split a large popcorn into two bags and put butter on one. The high schooler wasn't exactly trained in customer service, and he said that's just not the way it's done. But Mike wouldn't let it go. He asked the kid if he got another bag at the kiosk where they sell candy by the pound and put the popcorn in the bag himself, could he have butter on that? No doubt worn down, the kid agreed. I left the whole popcorn business in Mike's hands and went to the ladies' room.

When I came out, Mike did indeed have two bags of popcorn—a tiny one from the candy kiosk and a giant one. He handed me the tiny one. The big bag of popcorn had butter all over it. Basically, I got stiffed for a huge bag of popcorn I couldn't even enjoy.

- Nyla, New York, New York

The Chosen One

When I met my future husband, Len, I was dating other men, including a guy named Mark. In general, I felt that the guys I dated, although they had important jobs, became competitive when I talked about *my* own work experiences. I often deal with the most senior people in Fortune 500 companies and conduct offsite meetings in resorts around the world.

Len, who I met when I worked as a consultant at his company, was quite different. A widower with two children, he had been married to a woman who helped him develop his sensitivity to women. He called me every night after his children went to bed and asked how my day was. In contrast, Mark called on Wednesdays to plan for Saturday night dates. On Saturdays we "reported" how our weeks went.

With Len, it was "in the moment," with all the emotions and details. As I slowly shared my stories with him, I'd find that he was very supportive and encouraging, giving me more ideas as we talked. I always felt as if I was taken to another level with anything I shared. In contrast, with Mark, as I tested the waters—sharing my stories of the week—I found myself hearing cues to stop. My enthusiasm for my accomplishments went flat in his presence.

This contrast was a defining moment regarding the type of person I wanted to be around. Len and I have been married for ten years now, and we're still sharing and adding to each other's ideas.

Chris, Phoenix, Arizona

LOSER

Yo-Yo Dating

I met Tyler through a Speed-Dating event.

I thought we had a real match. Our first date lasted six hours. In the following weeks, we spent a lot of time together and talked on the phone every night. After six weeks, Tyler said he wanted to be exclusive. That sounded great. But I wondered if he had any other Speed Dates left.

"Actually, I have one last date," he said.

"So why don't we wait to be exclusive till after your date?" I offered.

He waved off my objections. "You don't have anything to worry about," he said. "Let's just say we're exclusive, and I've got this one last date."

It didn't make much sense, but I reluctantly agreed. His "last" date was scheduled for Sunday. The following Thursday we were to drive to New York City. We weren't technically going away together, but since we both had plans to be in the city, we decided to carpool.

We traded phone messages on Monday. We didn't talk on Tuesday. It seemed odd that we weren't connecting, because until then we'd talked every day. Wednesday night he called. We talked about nothing much for a while, and finally I asked, "So, how was your date?"

"Oh yeah," he dodged. "I've been meaning to talk to you. I *don't* want to be exclusive. The girl was nice, and I want to see her again.

I was stunned. "When were you going to tell me?" I demanded.

"I dunno. When it came up. Maybe during the drive. You knew I went on a date. You could have asked me."

"I just did ask you," I said, my voice icy.

"I've got to go. We'll talk more on the way to the city."

I decided to go by myself. When I called to let him know, I told him, "Look, it would have been fine if you'd said, 'I made a mistake about being exclusive.' But you were dishonest."

He actually asked, "Is *that* what you meant by honesty?"

- Skye, Cos Cob, Connecticut

Perfect First Date

Tom and I met on a double date with another couple who had fixed us up. On our first solo date I was supposed to meet him at 7 PM, but I was running late and didn't get to his apartment until close to 9. We headed to the movies. Afterward, we went out for hamburgers. We talked for a couple of hours, and I drove him back to his apartment.

We sat out front, and I waited for him to kiss me goodnight or even just give me a handshake. Something. He asked if I had to go home, and when I said I didn't, he suggested we go shoot some pool. At this point it was 1 AM. We shot pool for an hour or so. When I drove him home again, it was now 3 AM. He asked if we could do this again. He didn't give me a kiss. There was no physical contact—which was a *huge* plus, as just about every other guy I'd dated prior to him would have jumped me.

As I was about to leave he said, "Would you give me a call when you get home?"

I said, "That will be about an hour from now."

He replied, "That's not a problem. I just want to make sure you get home okay."

I drove off with a big smile on my face. Then I wondered if maybe he didn't make a move because he just wanted to be friends. I stopped off at a pay phone (this was way before cell phones) and called him. He asked if I was home already. I said no, but that I had a question. "Do you just like me as a friend?" He answered, "I have enough friends." When I got home, I was still smiling. I called him at 4 AM, and we stayed on the phone for another two hours. I knew he was the one.

- Sophia, Philadelphia, Pennsylvania

LOSER

Blind (Drunk) Date

I had been with one guy all through high school and wasn't sure how the whole casual dating thing worked. So while I was single and living in New York City, I wanted to see what it was about. I met a guy in a bar I hung out in on Sunday nights. He seemed cool, he worked in computers, he was tall and good looking, and he played pool.

The night of our date, we met up at the bar. He was in his work suit. But within an hour, his tie and shirt were loose, and he'd had four vodka shots. We were playing pool, and he was chasing me around the table trying to grab me. Then he announced that he wanted to go dancing or do "something wacky." Well, we never made it, because as soon as we walked outside he said he felt sick and wanted to crash. He looked extremely green.

I took him home, thinking this would be the one-night stand I'd heard so much about. After all, he'd been mauling me the entire night. Plus, I felt a little sorry for him. He seemed like a nice guy who just had some problems. But when we got upstairs, he'd had so much to drink, he just took off his pants and fell asleep on the bed. Of course, I got no sleep that night. I was afraid he was going to throw up all over my new sheets. And I'd heard stories about how people throw up in their sleep and choke. I worried that I'd have to take him to the emergency room, or that he'd die and then I'd have to explain what this strange guy was doing in my bed.

In the morning, we had a very uncomfortable breakfast at a coffee shop, then went our separate ways. What sucked was that I couldn't go back to the bar. I really liked that place, but I didn't want to risk running into him.

- Tanya, New York, New York

Double Your Pleasure . . .

I met my future husband, Bob, at Penn State when I was a freshman. He lived in my dorm, and I remember thinking, *Hey, this guy looks pretty normal and definitely very cute.* Our paths crossed, but we didn't date until the beginning of the next year. Then we went out one night, and we had a really good time for a first date. There was lots of talking. There was also lots of apricot brandy. He said he would call.

The next afternoon I was walking near Old Main, where there is a lot of student traffic. It was a beautiful day and who did I see up ahead but Bob walking straight toward me. As the distance between us shortened, I got kind of breathy with anticipation. He kept coming toward me, and I kept walking toward him, getting ready to dive into the new relationship. Then he passed me by without a word.

Mouth hanging open, I stopped in my tracks, not believing that this guy could play such a game. Then with my back up and my nerves on edge, I turned around and ran through the crowd after him. I hollered, "Hey, Brown. You snob! What's up?" At that, 'Hey Brown' turned around.

Something about him was all wrong. The face. The gesture. He looked the same, but somehow not the same.

It was Bob, but it wasn't Bob. This guy did not grin at me. He was cool, but a little standoffish and less sure of himself. When he said, "I'm sorry, do I know you?" I knew it definitely wasn't Bob. Then from the back of my apricot-brandied brain, I pulled out the existence of a "twin." Bob had mentioned his brother in the midst of miles of conversation the night before.

"You must know my brother," said Hey Brown, who later turned out to be named Steve.

Funny, but I think it was just then that I realized how very special Bob already was to me . . . in contrast to even his genetic match. Steve, who is very dear to me now, is just not Bob at all.

Marie, Tenafly, New Jersey

LOSER

Me . . . Not Me

I met a guy through Nerve.com. He was working on his PhD at Cornell University in Ithaca, New York, and I was in Manhattan. He emailed me, saying, "I know we're out of range for meeting up for coffee and dessert, but I had to tell you that I was taken by your picture from 200 miles away. I think you're beautiful."

Who could resist an opener like that?

We started emailing regularly and talked on the phone for two weeks. Then on his way to catch a plane in Baltimore, he stopped in New York City to see me. We wound up talking on my roof till 4 AM, at which point he drove off to Baltimore and just made his flight. On his way home, he stopped in New York to see me again.

My head was spinning. *Wow! This is very cool.* I never expected anything like this at all.

A week later, he slammed on the brakes. "I can't be distracted by a relationship now," he told me. "I'm studying for my PhD."

Stupidly, I held out hope. We still talked a lot and emailed back and forth. Then, a few months later, I got another email from him that said, "Hey, we haven't talked in a while, but I wanted to let you know that I started seeing someone. She's amazing, and funny how it happened—we met through Nerve.com. She's in New York City." And he proceeded to describe all these things that sounded just like me. Except . . . it wasn't me. He even told me how great their sex was.

Then he asked, "Since I'll be in New York City a lot, would you like to have lunch sometime?"

I told him I'd be really busy—every day.

- Carla, New York, New York

KEEPER

A December/May Romance

Adam and I met at work, but I wasn't interested in dating him. He was very nice, but he was also sixteen years younger than me. I even considered fixing him up with my daughter when she broke up with her boyfriend.

We were in the same office bowling league, and one afternoon I casually asked, "Why aren't you dating anyone?"

"I'm looking," he said.

"You know if you ever want to go to the movies or something, as friends, let me know."

He paused for about three seconds and said, "How about Thursday?"

At one point I asked him how old he thought I was, and he said 35. I told him the truth: I was 41. I really resisted this romance. I put up every barrier in the book. I made sure he knew I wasn't interested in having kids. Nothing seemed to faze him.

When he got a job offer in another town, I told him he should take advantage of it. We had been hanging out just as friends for about six weeks, and he was leaving the next day for his new job. He walked me to my door. I invited him in. *And he turned me down.* He kissed me on the cheek and said, "If I come in, I won't want to leave."

That's when I knew I wanted him as more than a friend. He could easily have taken advantage of me. The minute he walked away, I burst into tears.

It turned out that Adam was miserable at his new job and didn't stay there long. Shortly after that, when he asked me to marry him, I didn't even hesitate. Sure my friends thought I was out of my mind. But we were married just a few months later in 1994. I have been blessed.

- Lorraine, Middletown, New York

LOSER

The Next Best Thing to Being There

On the morning after the first night spent with a new (much younger) guy, I woke up to find my handsome, half-naked paramour reaching for the phone. Was he calling to order me flowers? Phoning all his exes to tell them to stop chasing him down, because he'd found the love of his life? No, he called his college roommate and shouted out, "Hey, guess what, man? I got a *girl* in my bed!"

- Susan, Hanover, New Jersey

And All That Jazz . . .

On our first date, Zach and I went for dinner at Il Radicchio in Washington, DC. Then we were supposed to see *The Garden of the Finzi-Continis,* but we were so into our conversation over dinner we were too late and ended up seeing another foreign film.

Afterward, it began to snow. It was the first snowfall and very romantic. I knew I wanted to see him again, but I wasn't sure if he just wanted to be friends. I was thinking maybe he'd want to go with me to see this jazz duo the next night. Not many people have heard of them—Tuck and Patti, a married couple who play romantic jazz. I took a chance and asked what he was doing the next day.

He answered, "Well, I debated asking you, but I have tickets to go see this jazz duo. Nobody really knows who they are. So I was going to take a friend."

I stopped dead in my tracks and said, "Tuck and Patti?"

He stopped, looked at me and smiled. I swear freakin' rockets went off. He said, "You know them?"

"I love them," I said.

"Then we're going."

That was it. I knew I would marry him.

- Lynn, Arlington, Virginia

LOSER

The Would-Be Cassanova

I met Alan in graduate school at Columbia. We didn't have any classes together, so I didn't know him well when he asked me out. He was smart. And he worked for a magazine I loved, so I wanted to hear how he got the job.

One night, we hit a few bars. Alan seemed interesting—and interested in me. Until he started talking about his "wandering eye." "I generally get tired of women within a few hours," he actually told me. "If the conversation is going nowhere, I start checking out other girls."

For a minute I thought this was an awkward way of complimenting me. His way of saying, I was different, interesting. Then he was off on another tangent about first-date sex. "It's such a turnoff if a woman wants to go to bed too quickly," he told me.

I tried to change the subject. And his attention evaporated. When I realized he was no longer listening, I decided to call it a night.

He insisted on walking me out, which I appreciated until I realized that our last stop was right across from his apartment. Oblivious to how he'd offended me, he was now trying to sweet talk me upstairs into bed.

"Alan, if I came up tonight, you wouldn't call me tomorrow," was my polite blowoff. Then I jumped into a cab and went home.

That was our only date. The next time I saw Alan, he was featured in a women's magazine sex survey. What really made me laugh was his reference to our date. He said one of the best things a women had ever said to him at the end of a date was, "If I came up tonight, you wouldn't call me tomorrow."

I couldn't believe he hadn't seen my blowoff for what it was. Amused, I called him. But as I left the message on his answering machine, I started cracking up.

He never called me back. But I didn't feel too badly, I figured that my uncontrollable laughter was a bit like his uncontrollable wandering eye.

- Andrea, Greenwich, Connecticut

KEEPER

He Was Cat Scanned!

I'm a "Love Me, Love My Kitties" kind of gal. So when a friend introduced me to Bruce, I wasn't sure if it was going to work out because right off the bat he said, "You know I don't really like cats. Every time I pet one it turns around and scratches me."

I decided I should introduce him to my cats before we got too involved. We were sitting on the couch one night, and wouldn't you know it, my shy cat Cricket came up and snuggled next to him. Without missing a beat, Bruce started to pet him. And then Mitzi came over and sprawled out on his lap. There was Bruce practically purring over my cats. My cats had met other boyfriends, but they never reacted to anyone else that way. Both cats just took to Bruce. When I looked over and saw this non-cat person snuggled up with *my* cats, I knew.

• Helena, Doylestown, Pennsylvania

Color Coordinated

A friend tried to fix me up with this guy who was a money manager on Wall Street. One of the things she told him about me was that I had reddish hair—I'm sort of a strawberry blonde. So he called me, and we were talking, having our first get-to-know-you conversation—we hadn't even met in person yet. Suddenly he blurted, "Hey, does your collar match your cuffs?"

Huh? I had no idea what he was talking about.

Then he explained it to me. He wanted to know whether my pubic hair was the same color as the hair on my head!

- Lauren, Hoboken, New Jersey

A Moving Story

I've had to move several times because of work, and each time moving my bedroom furniture—particularly a very heavy futon—was a logistical nightmare. This time I was moving from Connecticut to New Jersey, where I was going to be living with a few other people—including two men whom I hadn't yet met. I wondered, *How was I going to move my futon from hell?* In general, I'm not a damsel in distress. I'm very capable. But this futon was just too freaking heavy!

I got two kind souls who lived in the neighborhood to help carry all my furniture down to the curb for me. I didn't have room for all the pieces, so I left the futon on the curb—half hoping someone would take it! When I got to New Jersey, my new roommate Ben asked if I needed any help.

"Well, there is this *one* piece," I answered.

His immediate response was, "No problem."

We drove all the way back to Connecticut, and the futon was still there. He could barely fit it in his trunk. We had to tie it down with a bungee cord.

It turned out that this was just the way Ben was—and still is. I was so impressed that he offered to help. We were friends for a while. But now we've been married eleven years.

- Laney, Cape May, New Jersey

LOSER

Time Warp

Where you live says a lot about who you are and where you're at in your life. So I was really shocked when I finally got to see my boyfriend Wayne's apartment. We always hung out at my place, and when I got to his place, I could see why he never wanted me to come over.

I had guessed that he wasn't into getting married and that he had a fear of commitment. Sure enough, when I got to his apartment, I got all of those vibes. His place had no life in it. I went into his kitchen, and there were literally sprouts growing out of the sink, coming up through the holes in the drain. The bathroom—I was afraid to use it—was completely gross, like it had never been cleaned. The whole scene was too Miss Haversham-ish, frozen in time, like nothing had been changed in years. There were books and papers piled up all over the place along with old clothes and shoes he'd bought fifteen years ago. The whole place was just creepy, and I couldn't bring myself to see him again.

- Lynn, Los Angeles, California

KEEPER

The Price Is Right

My husband and I met at Oberlin College in Ohio. I was a sophomore and he was a senior. When he graduated and moved to Boston to go to graduate school, we tried to have a long-distance relationship. Norm was known by all to be very frugal. He watches his pennies; he cuts coupons. When he first moved to Beantown, he suggested we *only* talk on Wednesday and Sunday when the rates were low. That's just who he is. I respected that, but I really wanted to visit him. One night I said nervously, "I really want to come and see you, but I can't afford it. Will you pay for half of my plane ticket?" Before I even finished asking he said, "Of course."

You have to understand how he was with money at that time. His coming up with $100 so I could fly out from Oberlin was a really big deal for him. But he did it, and that meant a lot.

• June, Boston, Massachusetts

LOSER

The Price Is Wrong

My boyfriend Tony offered to fix the front gate for the home owners association in my housing development. The association paid him to fix the gate, but hadn't reimbursed him for the paint he'd bought to finish it. He wanted to go to the association officers and demand his $2.50. I was so embarrassed. But his cheapness finally drove me over the edge when the 8-year-old boy next door asked Tony to fix his bicycle tire for him . . . and he wanted to charge the kid five bucks to do it.

- Janice, Boca Raton, Florida

KEEPER

He Made My Mom Really Happy

My family is fraught with food allergies, all from my father's side. This has always been very frustrating for my mother, who loves to cook and feed people. Get us together for Thanksgiving and almost no one can eat the turkey or the stuffing. So the first time I brought my boyfriend home to meet my parents, my mother was excited. My sister had introduced us, so my mother called *her* ahead of time to find out what Leo could eat. "I think he eats everything," my sister said.

My mother was so happy. She just kept bringing out dish after dish, and Leo ate it. Afterward he sat around like a stuffed pig. I didn't think he could eat another bite. Then mom came out of the kitchen and said, "Would you like some of my homemade candy?"

Leo took a deep breath (I didn't know what he was going to say) and sighed. "Would you like another son?"

From that moment on he was definitely a Keeper—for my mother as well.

- Mary Ann, Wheeling, West Virginia

LOSER

He Didn't Even Know I Had a Mom

I dated a guy who was highly intelligent and generally kindhearted, but he was just one of those guys who talked a lot about himself and never seemed interested in my life. After we'd been dating for several months it struck me that I knew everything about his family: his mom's recent death from cancer, his father's starting to date again, his brother and his brother's girlfriend. He, however, didn't even know my parents' names or what they did for a living. I don't think he even knew how many siblings I had or what their names were. His self-absorption eventually turned me off.

- Allison, Silver Spring, Maryland

He Even Spoils My Siblings

I think I realized right from the start that Frank was a Keeper. We started dating when I was just 16 and he was 18. I am the third of six children and was always a "mother hen" to my two little sisters and little brother. Frank fell right in with spoiling them. When he came over, he would drop his change onto the floor of his car and tell them that they could keep whatever coins they found. They would often come along with us on fun trips to the beach, amusement parks, or for ice cream. Whenever a new Disney movie came out, Frank always offered to take them to see it.

Almost thirty years have passed since then, and Frank is still spoiling "the three little kids." My youngest sister now lives in Pennsylvania, a three-hour drive away. Whenever I mention that my sister sounds lonely or she's had a bad day, Frank will say we should go and see her. These visits are sometimes just a trip for lunch, with us bringing the New York deli food that she can't get near her. He's always looking for ways he can still spoil them.

- Jeanne, Babylon, New York

LOSER

Joke's on . . . You

I was dating Keith, the editor of our college newspaper, at the end of our sophomore year. Before summer vacation, it was all fabulous and amazing. But when I came back in the fall, he was sort of passive. I didn't realize it at first, but he was sending out "break up with me" signals because he didn't have the balls to do it himself.

Everything came to a head on Halloween weekend. My sister was visiting, and about eight of us were going to dinner and then to a costume party. During dinner, my boyfriend's best friend was telling a joke. He'd just told it to me, and I broke in, blurting, "Is this the one where . . ." and accidentally spoiled the punch line.

Keith looked at me, and in front of everyone—including my sister, whom he should have been trying to impress—scolded, "Debbie, that's the third time you've done that today. Don't do that again!"

I just sat there openmouthed. Later that night I dumped him. It was pretty funny, actually. He was a big guy, 6'3", and he was in drag that night—lipstick, fishnets, the works. When I told him, you should have seen the look on his pretty face.

- Debbie, Ann Arbor, Michigan

KEEPER

A Modest Proposal

I met my husband, Andy, at, of all places, a Jewish singles weekend at Virginia Beach. I had come down from New York with two friends. There must have been about 500 of us, all between the ages of 20 and 50. At first I was mostly rolling my eyes and thinking, *What am I doing here?* Soon, though, I met a few guys, so I was feeling a little like Scarlett O'Hara with several men clustered around me. But I felt like I really struck gold when I met Andy on the line for dinner that first night, both of us waiting for the salmon.

There was something very genuine and unassuming about him. I found him natural and without barriers. I talked to a lot of people that weekend, but I kept coming back to Andy. The last night we took a walk on the beach.

"Have you ever been married?" he asked as we strolled.

I hadn't.

"Would you *like* to be married?"

Men are often uncertain about commitment, so I was surprised to hear Andy say this. Usually it's the woman who wants commitment. To have it expressed by Andy, a man in his forties, I thought was a really, really good sign. We wanted the same things!

He was from Bethesda, Maryland, and he flew up to visit me the next weekend. We were married very soon after.

- Clare, Bethesda, Maryland

LOSER

A Swift Refusal

During dinner at a fancy restaurant, one of the waiters caught my eye. He was Turkish and beautiful. A few days later, I tracked him down at the restaurant and asked him out for dinner. He loved that I called him! When he picked me up, he immediately kissed me hello—and stuck his tongue down my throat. That's not how *I* say hello. I didn't even get *hello* out.

Once we got to the restaurant—Turkish, which I thought was cool—it was like we were on fast forward. I'm a writer, and I mentioned that I was trying to research a story in Istanbul. He immediately offered me the use of his family's house there. As the conversation went on, he told me that his family was always asking him why he hadn't met a "nice American girl" yet. He mentioned that his sister was getting married in Turkey and invited me along. Then he started talking about how great things would be if *we* got married and had kids. Our entrees hadn't even arrived yet.

After dinner I'd had enough. I told him to take me home. When he called the next day to ask when we could get together again, I told him I wasn't interested, that he was too forward. He didn't get it. He kept saying, "But you called me!"

- Georgianna, Berkeley, California

KEEPER

Take Two Echinacea . . .

I met my second husband on a blind date just six months after leaving my first husband. I had a lot of trepidation about making any kind of commitment. I thought of Walt as just someone to date once in a while.

Flash forward a few months. I was working for a large accounting firm, and my department was going to have a party after work. Unfortunately, I had a really lousy cold and went home early. Walt called just to say hi and to ask how I was doing. I told him I had a cold and thought that was the end of it. About an hour later the bell rang. There was Walt with flowers, herbal tea, and some natural cold remedies he had picked up at a health food store. I'm a vegan and never take regular medicine. Even though up until this point we had just been casually dating, I couldn't believe how thoughtful he was and how well he knew me. He had been paying attention. My first husband could not handle me being sick or needy. It sent him over the edge. If I sent him out for aspirin, he would show up hours later.

- Linda, Flint, Michigan

LOSER

No Tea . . . or Sympathy

My husband was an insecure guy who needed symbolic indications of his status as a "man." One of the things he stuck on was that he wouldn't do anything "feminine," like cook, if I was around. I think he was afraid that if he picked up a pot, his balls would shrivel and fall off.

On this particular occasion I was home sick in bed, and my husband, a law student at the time, was in the next room studying. I wanted a cup of tea to settle my stomach. I didn't ask him to make me tea, just to put the water on so that when it boiled, I'd only have to get up once and make the tea myself. He refused. He wouldn't touch the kettle.

- Samantha, Brooklyn, New York

KEEPER

Roses Would Smell As Sweet

My doctor was treating me for gastrointestinal problems, and my medication often caused me to pass horrible smelling gas—you know, the silent but deadly kind. One night when my boyfriend and I were out, I was particularly afflicted. I was trying to be strategic about dropping these little "bombs" and hoping I was keeping things under control. Suddenly Dan looked at me. "Did you just fart?"

I turned deep red, then started apologizing all over the place while explaining about the medicine. Dan shook his head like he didn't care, took my hand and said, "It's all roses to me, hon."

- Janet, Daytona Beach, Florida

LOSER

Picky, Picky, Picky

A few years back I placed a personal ad in a newspaper. The man who responded was in his late forties, a scientist working at a pharmaceutical company in the Bay Area. He seemed well educated—he had a PhD from Berkeley—and very nice. I thought, *He'd be an interesting guy*. We decided to meet at this coffee shop in Palo Alto to get to know each other.

We never got past the first date. He picked his nose the entire time. Gross.

- Rebecca, Palo Alto, California

KEEPER

An Officer *and* a Gentleman

My husband and I were high school sweethearts. In grade school I knew him as "the boy who stepped on my fingers during assemblies." He moved away, and then returned just before high school. He was in the band and I was on the dance team, and we used to meet up before the school year began to rehearse. We just started dating and never quit.

At the end of high school I had plans to attend college in Washington, DC, and he decided to join the Marines as a principal trumpeter. I wondered how going through boot camp and moving around would affect our relationship, but he had *no* doubts whatsoever. I really questioned whether a long-distance relationship could work.

Just before he went to boot camp, he drove down to school to surprise me. He gave me a promise ring. No matter what, he pledged, our distance would never cause the demise of our relationship, and this was a small token representing his intention to marry me and spend the rest of his life with me. I was thrilled. I have about 300 letters from his three months in boot camp.

Even though we did spend four years apart while I was in college, somehow he has *always* made me feel that we are together.

We were married in August 2003. I have no doubt that he is my soul mate. He kept his promise, and I never take off his ring.

- Kelly, Washington, DC

LOSER

A Girl in Every Port

Mike and I were 17 when we met at a church dance. Our parents had been good friends long before we even met. He was headed for the Marines boot camp. But we talked on the phone the whole time he was away. Right before he came home on leave we finally said, "I love you." And then he'd call every five minutes, saying, "I love you, I love you, I miss you, I miss you."

It wasn't long before he asked me to marry him. We picked out rings when he came home and started planning the wedding. But after he'd gone back to boot camp, his mom called my mom and said, "My son can't marry your daughter. He got another girl pregnant."

When I called him about it, he naturally denied getting anyone pregnant. But I didn't believe him and called off the wedding.

- Janet, Boise, Idaho

KEEPER

It Was Fate

I was living in Israel. I'm an artist, and during a trip to London for an exhibition of my work, a friend took me to see a fortune-teller. This lady took my ring and held it in her hand. She told me I would meet the love of my life in the next few months, and I would be with him for more than twenty years. She said I would have to cross an ocean to meet him. I asked her, "How will I know him?" She told me he would be wearing light blue shoes. Since I knew I was going back to Israel, all I could think of was that men in Israel *never* wear light blue shoes—it's not macho!

I went back to Israel and forgot all about the fortune-teller. A few months later, I was invited by a friend to go to a party. I didn't have a car, so my friend asked his friend Marty to pick me up. When Marty showed up on time, I was impressed because most people got lost coming to my apartment for the first time. He asked to see my art, and I could tell he really appreciated my work. We had so much to talk about, and were so interested in each other, that we didn't get to the party until about midnight.

The very next day he came back and took me for a walk on the beach. I looked down at the sand and there they were—light blue deck shoes. That's when the prediction all came back to me. Without really thinking, I told Marty about the prediction. He was quite the entrenched bachelor at the time and turned very pale!

We are married twenty-four years now. I like to joke that it was the fortune-teller who knew I had a Keeper! I only wish I had thought to save those shoes.

- Rose, Los Angeles, California

LOSER

Not in the Stars

I fell for this very cute lawyer who was also an astrologer. We made a date, and he showed up at my apartment with a surprise for me—he'd done our charts. Unfortunately, he had determined that we were totally incompatible and that I would smother him. I guess it didn't matter that I'm not the smothering type. But rather than call me up and let me know that we were incompatible so I could make other plans, he showed me the chart, explained why we couldn't go out, stayed another hour or so and then left.

- Lara, Sedona, Arizona

KEEPER

The Quiet Man

I met my husband when he answered my personal ad—"Green-eyed lady seeks kind, intelligent male companion." We met on a Sunday for lunch near his office in Chinatown. I thought he was nice, but there were no rockets or bells going off. After lunch he asked if I would like a lift back to Brooklyn, where we both lived. I said sure but that I needed to stop off at Pearl Paint, an art supply store, to get a sketch pad for an art class. I really expected him to say, "It's been nice meeting you. Bye." But instead he said, "I'll go pull the car around."

He walked me over to Pearl Paint and showed me where to meet him. It's a huge store, and it took me a while to find what I needed. When I was finally done, I came running out with my package, expecting him to be impatient and fuming, like my ex-husband. He was just standing there waiting with a sweet expression. I thought, *Boy, this guy would make a fantastic husband*. I didn't set out to marry him, but I could see he had lots of potential. When he dropped me off at home, I could tell he wanted to see me again. So I took his hand and said, "I'd like to get together again." He told me later that he would have called me anyway.

- Janet, Brooklyn, New York

LOSER

My Little Ding-a-Ling

I'd just come off of another relationship. You know how you're feeling like you're not attractive anymore and maybe you don't still got it? So I might have rushed in a little bit with the next guy. But he was 6'4", good looking, a runner, he drove a sports car, he shot quail—it was all part of the I'm a Macho Guy thing.

After a few dates, though, I realized he was a bit of an exaggerator. Before I'd been to his place he told me he had a gym in his apartment. I work out regularly, and I thought, *Wow! A gym! Amazing!* So then I actually got to his apartment, and well . . . it was one of those little machines that you order from QVC. You can do a situp. Or you can pull a band. It wasn't a gym at all—it was a piece of exercise equipment.

And one night we were walking in Greenwich Village after a date, and he said, "See that building? I own that building." Well . . . it turns out he didn't actually *own* the building. He and a few friends had invested in a few apartments in the building.

Unfortunately, that wasn't all he exaggerated. We were in his apartment one night. One thing was leading to another, and we were all ready to go. I must say, while I've had very few meetings with the male member, I've seen enough. I know that there are a variety. You have your extra long, your skinny, your fat. But I did not know, until that moment, that they came in . . . petite.

It was really unbelievable. At full attention, ready to go, it was about the size of a little salt shaker.

I actually slept with him a second time just to get another look.

- Alin, Southport, Connecticut

KEEPER

Lean on Me

I moved to Washington, DC, about two years ago with my roommate Amanda and her friend Jimmy, who was from her hometown. Our first night there, Jimmy threw a moving-in party for us and for the two guys who were moving into the town house with him. I thought one of his new roommates, Andy, was really cute and sweet, and later found out he thought the same about me. Since we were all new to the area we hung out a lot.

After being in DC for about a month I ran into some heavy family problems.

I had only been with Andy for a few weeks. In fact, I don't even think we had technically been on a date alone yet. But I needed a shoulder to cry on and didn't think twice about calling him. It's safe to say that with most guys, if a girl they had only known for a few weeks called them up crying and upset about her dysfunctional family, they would go running. But Andy just listened and consoled me and held me while I had a meltdown. I never once had the feeling that I could be jeopardizing our relationship. That was the moment I knew he was definitely a Keeper.

More than a year and a half later we are living together, and I can't imagine a future without him. And he has stayed as wonderful and understanding about all my quirks and problems as he was in those first few weeks.

- Mindy, Washington, DC

LOSER

Animal House Redux

I'd been seeing Josh for about six months. It wasn't very serious, but I liked him a lot. That all changed at a Fourth of July party. We'd gone to the party separately, and when I got to the roof of the apartment building where everyone was hanging out, there was a crowd of about fifty people surrounding Josh, watching him make out with another girl. And they were egging him on, like a bad fraternity party, yelling, "Do her! Do her! Do her!"

- Claire, New York, New York

Good in Bed

Soon after I had a mastectomy, I met an appealing man at a singles event. We dated for a while and our relationship deepened, but I was reluctant to tell him about my surgery and even more reluctant to go to bed with him. In his easygoing and pragmatic manner he acknowledged my unease, and without a moments hesitation simply suggested that I keep my bra on the first time we made love. I did, and we have been together for a very long time.

- Shelly, Silver Spring, Maryland

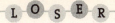

For I Have Sinned

On a trip to Mexico, I looked up a guy I dated when I'd lived there briefly. In the time I'd been away, he'd turned into a Jesus freak. He told me he'd seen the light. Nonetheless, we got together again—intimately—which he shouldn't have been doing, having "seen the light."

When I woke up in the morning, he was kneeling by the bed, praying for forgiveness. I've never been so offended in my life. I got dressed quickly and beat it out of there. I never saw him again.

- Monica, San Diego, California

Cooler Heads Prevailed

A good friend of mine introduced me to the man I'm married to today. But instead of being glad of the match, she switched gears and became very jealous and tried to break us up. She even went as far as warning me that if I should stay with Colin he would really hurt me. Though it was clear my girlfriend was trying to sabotage our relationship, Colin just kept his cool. He tried to see things from her point of view. He pointed out to me that she was insecure about losing me, and that she must have been desperate to behave the way she did. She said some awful things, but instead of getting insecure himself or becoming mean, Colin took the high road. I thought he was pretty mature for a 22-year-old guy. I knew at that moment that he was no ordinary man. So in my book, he's a Keeper. As for my friend, though I appreciate her introducing us, *she* is the Loser.

- Pam, Washington, DC

LOSER

Hot to Trot

Gene and I were living together in Boston. He was a bartender, a few years younger than me, free-spirited and very handsome—so handsome I was constantly amazed that I was actually with him.

Things between us were going really well. I remember at one point a mutual friend was going through a breakup. Gene and I talked about how great it was that we had this nice, solid relationship.

Then I spent a week in New York City, visiting college friends. Gene called me nightly to check in—you know, like, "Hi, I love you, hope you're having fun." One night I hadn't heard from him yet, so I called him. We had an answering machine, but this was back in the late 1980s, so it wasn't one that let you call in and check messages; you could only *leave* messages.

But by some quirk of fate, when I called, the machine malfunctioned and rather than record my message, it started playing back all of the messages that had been recorded, including one from my good friend Simone to Gene thanking him for the lovely night they'd spent together. It was a total fluke that I found out he cheated—I'd have never known if the answering machine hadn't done that.

Naturally they denied everything. I still broke up with Gene.

P.S. Months later I got a call from Simone. It turns out that after she and Gene started dating, he cheated on her! She wanted to know if we could be friends since we'd both been screwed over by the same guy. Ha!

- Bonnie, New York, New York

KEEPER

King of Hearts

Years ago I worked as an editor in an office on the sixth floor of a big office building. My desk faced a large window and often, while thinking or talking on the phone, I'd entertain myself by gazing out my window. I was fascinated by an office on the fifth floor in the building across the street that I could peer right down into. The office was lined with bookcases and had one of those fabulous sliding library ladders running along the bookcases. Being in the book business, I coveted that office. I often worked late and began to notice that the gent whose office I longed for also burned the midnight oil. So as I was sitting at my desk late one evening, the only beacon of light that reached me from outside came from the office with the library ladder. It dawned on me that those were the Barnes & Noble corporate offices. Of course, another book person.

A few weeks later at lunch I ran into an old friend who was an independent bookseller. We stopped to chat, and my friend introduced me to the gentleman with him. I didn't think much about it until later that day, as I gazed across the street and realized that the fellow I'd met on the sidewalk was the very guy whose office I loved. It seems he'd been watching me watch him and recognized me immediately. While I watched, he got up from his desk, walked over to the window, and waved.

The next day our mutual friend, the independent bookseller, called to ask if it was all right to pass on my phone number. I said sure, and Mr. Barnes & Noble called the next day. We played phone tag for a few days until I propped a sign in my window that said, "Will you have dinner with me on Friday night?" The phone rang immediately with him saying, "Yes."

A few days later it was Halloween. When I looked out the window to his office across the street, there was a cardboard Casper the Ghost propped up—with a little red heart drawn in.

• Milly, Chicago, Illinois

LOSER

Joker's Wild

I was dating a guy who had a bizarre sense of humor. *Everything* was always a big joke to him. One night we were out to dinner, and he sneezed. Only he didn't *just* sneeze. He thought it would be funny—as he was sneezing—to flip back in his chair, taking the tablecloth, all the food, everything with him. The other diners around us just kind of stared. I thought we should make a timely exit. I didn't see him after that. He was just too bizarre.

- Bernadette, Los Angeles, California

KEEPER

High and Dry

Right after I met Ted I had to have bunion surgery. It sounds silly, but it turned out to be a painful and difficult recovery. In addition to having a cast and needing to walk on crutches, I was told not to get my cast wet, no matter what. I had the fear of God put in me that if it got wet they would have to redo the procedure. Ted came to visit almost every night. After a week I decided I could make it to the movie theater in the neighborhood on my crutches. When we came out of the theater it was raining. I was terrified about navigating the two blocks home in the rain. Ted said, "Wait a minute. I'll go get you a plastic bag."

So he went to the deli on the corner and we put the bag on my leg. I said, "You know it doesn't quite cover the whole thing." So he went back to the deli for another plastic bag. I was still worried. I made him go back yet again. It took him three trips to the deli and three plastic bags before I felt comfortable. He never complained, made a face, or tried to talk me out of it.

- Rita, Riverdale, New York

LOSER

All Washed Up

Friends of mine threw a dinner party to introduce me to Glenn. I was an art history major in college, and he's a curator at a New York art museum. They thought it would be a great match. It wasn't.

Before we went to sit down to dinner, he used the bathroom. I used it after him. Let me be clear: He did not wash his hands. The sink was bone dry.

At dinner we were passing the food around. My friends served swordfish, but when the platter reached Glenn, the serving fork was missing. He used his hands to put the swordfish on his plate—then offered to help me with mine. I was totally repulsed, thinking about where his hands had been.

- Susanne, New York, New York

KEEPER

Swept Away for the Afternoon

I've long admired a certain pediatrician who I always considered my professional role model. Listening to me talk about him for years and wanting to give me a very special birthday gift, my husband wrote a letter to this esteemed "celebrity," telling him of my admiration and asking if he'd meet with me at his convenience. He assured the famous physician that he would keep their correspondence secret, never to be divulged if he were unable to meet me. Surprisingly, the humble and somewhat perplexed man agreed to a visit.

On my birthday my husband captured me at my office for the four-hour drive to Harvard, where, to my thorough delight, he delivered me to the home of none other than T. Berry Brazelton, the father of developmental pediatrics and my personal hero. After the introductions were made, my husband offered to walk the family dog in the snow so that Dr. Brazelton and I could sip tea and share the most amazing afternoon of my professional career. My jaw still drops when I think of all my husband did to arrange this and when I saw the magnificent smile on Dr. Brazelton's face as I later embraced my husband in gratitude.

- Polly, New York, New York

LOSER

Gunning for a Good Time

One night Todd and I were in bed when he leaned over to get what I thought was a condom from the nightstand because we were about to have sex. But instead of a condom, he pulled out . . . a gun, and laid it on the nightstand.

"Like it?" he asked.

"Not on the nightstand I don't." I was pretty unnerved. *Was it loaded?* I didn't even want to know. "Put it away," I insisted.

Apparently it turned him on to have the gun there. He actually wanted to use the gun as an implement, à la Monica and the cigar.

I could not get out of the apartment fast enough. I just put on my clothes and ran.

- Carole, Huntington, New York

KEEPER

If You Think I'm Sexy . . .

My husband and I have been happily married for seven years. I knew he was a Keeper when, despite listening to me vent about how exasperated I was with the slew of blind dates I'd gone on, he *still* wanted to accept a blind date with me. We had been fixed up by a mutual friend, and we spoke on the phone before we met in person. I told him how annoyed I was with men telling me how handsome they were, only to show up for a date to find some nerd waiting for me wearing highwaters and looking like he'd just crawled up out of the basement! I made it ridiculously clear that I couldn't tolerate one more self-embellishing jerk. I explained that if he misrepresented himself to me, I wouldn't hesitate to leave as soon as I saw him. When I asked him what he looked like, he simply said that his mother thought he was nice looking. How could I argue with that?

When I met him, my first thought was, *Okay, his mother is right. He is cute*. He wasn't the least bit nervous as far as I could tell. I admired how unperturbed and amused he seemed by my brashness. His interest in meeting me, despite my obvious reservations, revealed a confidence in himself, which to this day I still find very sexy.

- Reva, Madison, Wisconsin

LOSER

Up, Up and No Way

I was totally in love with Matt. He was beautiful, this dark, cool type who'd go to bars on a Saturday with a book and drink. He was smart and sweet, and made me realize that nice guys aren't dorks. We had great conversations. I wanted to be with him every waking moment.

The problem was, we'd dated for three months and still hadn't had sex. We both had two roommates, so the logistics could be a little difficult. But any time I would try to initiate sex, he'd say, "The timing isn't right." There was always some excuse. I'm not some huge sex fiend, but it had been *three months*. Finally he said, "I want to make love to you, but it should be special." I was thrilled.

We planned a romantic getaway weekend at Mohunk Mountain House in New Paltz, New York. After dinner on our first night we went back to our room. Everything was all romantic, we were starting to make love, and then . . . he stopped. Completely.

"Our rhythm's not right. We're not in sync," he said.

And that was the end of sex for the whole weekend.

Initially I couldn't figure out what was going on. Then it dawned on me. He couldn't get it up. It was unfortunate, but he wouldn't even entertain the idea that he had a problem. A few months later I had the chance to talk with another girl he dated. She said they never had sex either.

- Brett, New York, New York

KEEPER

Chemistry 101

I'm an athlete, I coach basketball, I'm generally aggressive. Basically I'm not a real "girly" type. I go back and forth about how forward I should be if someone appeals to me. As independent as I am—I speak my own mind, run my own business—I would still like a Prince Charming to take the lead and say, "You're amazing, let's see where this goes."

After a really bad divorce I spent two solid years alone, by choice. About the time when I was ready for another relationship, a good friend invited me to a focus group. I sat on a couch during the slide presentation. This guy Jim practically dove to be next to me. In the dim lighting I thought his hair was blond and maybe he was in his late twenties. (I'm 37.) I looked down, and he was wearing these amazing shoes. I immediately characterized them as gay footwear. Even though there was chemistry between us—he was sitting really close to me—I decided I had enough gay friends.

Then he leaned over, and I could see serious crow's-feet. Ah, he wasn't in his twenties after all; he was gray, not blond; and he wore glasses. When he stood, I realized he was about 6'3". So I flicked my "on" switch. After intermission we made eye contact, and it was clear he was interested. He leaned over and put both hands on my knee and said—I will never forget this as long as I live—"I really feel something is going on here. I'd love to spend more time with you and see what happens." He *says* I replied, "That could be arranged." Things got crazy and terrific real fast.

What was wonderful was that he was absolutely direct and sensitive to me. He understood that I was vulnerable, but he went for it. This "first moment" thing can be really difficult. He could see me pull away but, as he explained later that night, "The woman who invited us had issued the order that we should ask for what we wanted. I was just doing what I was supposed to do." Nice.

- Margie, Baltimore, Maryland

LOSER

Woo Is Me

I was working as a secretary in the Harvard Business School when one of the PhD candidates invited me to his house for dinner. We'd gone out once, someplace where we really couldn't talk much, so I didn't feel like I knew him that well.

When I got to his house, it was like a scene from a Doris Day/Rock Hudson movie, where he's always trying to get her into bed. All the lights were dimmed, he had candles everywhere, and had laid out a platter with brie and grapes and wine. There was a fire going, and—if you can believe it—a white bearskin run right in front of the fireplace! Plus, he gave me a book of very sexual, romantic poems by the lesbian poet Adrienne Rich—and circled all the sexually graphic ones. When he offered to massage my back, all I could think was, *He's moving too fast*. It was like a bad joke right out of *Saturday Night Live*.

Maya, Boston, Massachusetts

KEEPER

You Got Me, Babe

I had a rough divorce and was raising my daughter alone when I met Anthony. Things happened pretty fast. We started to talk about marriage, but we hadn't set a date. Then in December 1999, I was diagnosed with breast cancer. It became clear I was going to need a mastectomy followed by chemo. So I sat him down and said that maybe we shouldn't plan on getting married just yet because this changed everything. He just looked at me and said, "Honey, this doesn't change a thing." We were married in June 2000, and now we are both fighting my breast cancer.

- Sydney, Macon, Georgia

LOSER

Cold Comfort

I was meeting my (now ex-) husband and his parents for dinner at the end of a long, traumatic day. My cousin had had a breakdown, and when I'd gone to her apartment a few days earlier, I'd found her three children living in squalor. I'm a physician, and I immediately called Family Services to get the children out of there. That day I had been in court petitioning for temporary custody. It was an emotional day, and I was completely drained. By the time I joined my husband at the table with his parents, I was nearly in tears.

I leaned over and whispered to him that it had been a rough day and that I could use a hug. My rigid, cold surgeon husband just looked at me and said, "I don't think this is the place for that kind of display."

- Faye, Honolulu, Hawaii

KEEPER

All in the Family

Robert and I were set up by mutual friends and had our first date during Thanksgiving week. I was pleasantly surprised when there appeared to be an immediate spark between us.

In mid-December my parents left for a vacation. But the day before Christmas I received an urgent call from my mother telling me that my father had suffered a massive heart attack. It was uncertain whether he would survive, and I needed to get on the next plane. I was devastated and not thinking clearly. But Robert seemed to know exactly what to do. He assisted me with all the arrangements, drove me to the airport, and contacted me regularly while I was away, comforting me by telephone. Although we could not spend New Year's together, he made it a point to call me at midnight to wish my family and me well.

When I was ready to come home, Robert insisted on meeting me at the airport. My father was unable to travel, and my parents couldn't come back home for several months. Robert made sure that he was always available to assist in any way he could. In what was a very difficult hour of my life, he came through for me . . . and he hardly knew me. He was behaving just like a family member. You learn so much about people in crisis situations. I knew deep in my heart that here was a Keeper.

- Wanda, Bronx, New York

LOSER

Clothes Call

My father had just called me at work to tell me that my grandmother, who'd been very ill, was not going to last much longer, probably not more than another day or so. I wanted to go up to New Haven to help my father and say good-bye to my grandmother. I called my boyfriend Paul immediately and asked him to come over right after work. First thing in the morning I wanted to leave for New Haven. By the time Paul arrived, I was still freaking out, but my father had called again to tell me that my grandmother had stabilized and the situation was no longer as urgent. Somewhat relieved, I told Paul that we could wait to leave until later the following day.

At that news Paul started screaming at me, "Why didn't you call me and tell me I didn't have to rush up? I could have gone home to change out of my suit!"

That's right. His suit. We had a huge fight because I didn't call him to tell him that the crisis had passed, and now he was stuck in his suit. I was standing there with my mouth hanging open, thinking, *Is he kidding? Does he not get this?*

- Lisa, New York, New York

KEEPER

He Will Always Pave the Way for Me

Ken, who's pretty athletic, is a wonderful skier and very patient. We were skiing and there were some really big turns and no trails. Suddenly there was this bunch of trees, and all I could think of was Sonny Bono! When I told Ken that I was sure that tree had my name on it, he said without hesitation, "Hop on my back." (Luckily I am small.) He skied me back to safety down the mountain. It would have been cool to watch us go down, but I had my eyes closed the entire time.

- Dana, Tampa, Florida

LOSER

Cold Shoulder

I joined a bunch of friends in renting a winter ski house, even though I don't ski. I was taking lessons—progressing very slowly—when I started to date one of the guys in the house.

One weekend Russell suggested we ski together. I warned him I didn't really know how to ski, but he said not to worry and that he would teach me. The next thing I knew we were going up the mountain—I mean *up*! I was terrified on the ski lift. Once at our destination, which felt like the top of the Alps, Russell told me to start to ski. When he saw how bad I was, he remarked, "Gee, you really suck. See you at the bottom."

He skiied off and left me literally frozen with fear, my skis pointed down the mountain. I had my poles planted in the snow and was sure if I moved at all I would go flying down the slope. I finally flopped down in the snow, took off my skis and *walked* sideways—inch by inch—down the slope until I got to a ski lift. When I did get to the bottom, Russell couldn't figure out why I gave him the "cold" shoulder.

- Lee, Philadelphia, Pennsylvania

KEEPER

Thanks for the Memories

My good friend Terry wanted to fix me up with a widower she knew. She had been really good friends with his wife who died of a brain tumor. I was divorced with three kids and not interested. She kept saying, "You've really got to meet this guy." I kept saying I didn't want to meet *anybody*. Finally she said, "You guys don't need to meet, just email each other." So we did, for months. Then we worked up to talking on the phone.

A few months later I finally agreed to meet him—with conditions. He didn't pick me up. We met at a well-lit public place. The next time we went out for dinner and we drove in separate cars. Finally I asked myself if this was a guy I wanted to bring into my house. He was.

On our first "grown-up" date—where he came to the house and picked me up—we went to see *Meet the Parents*. I don't think he really wanted to see it, but he agreed. This guy kept the tickets and had them laminated! Soon after that date, he presented them to me. And as soon as the movie came out on tape, he bought two copies, one for each of us. How could I not want to keep him?

- Betty, Long Island, New York

LOSER

Come Again?

I met this guy on a flight from Phoenix to New York City. He was a stockbroker in his early twenties—gorgeous, tall, buff, really smart and funny. We chatted the whole time on the plane. I thought he was adorable.

We made plans to go out to dinner a week later. But when he came to pick me up at my apartment, he said he was tired and would much rather stay in. I was cool with that, so we ordered a pizza.

Then he started taking off his clothes. Only he did it so slowly and casually that I didn't realize what was going on.

First, he asked if he could hang up his jacket. *Sure.* We talked for a while, then he said, "Do you mind if I get more comfortable?" I wasn't sure what he meant, but said okay. He took off his shirt. *That* was a little bizarre. But he was wearing a tanktop undershirt, so I figured, *Odd, but all right.*

So we're sitting at the coffee table on the floor of my living room eating the pizza when suddenly he stands up and takes off his pants, gets another hanger and hangs them up. Then he moves in to kiss me. I'm like, "Whoa! What are you doing? You're moving *way* too fast. I don't know what you're thinking, but I'm not going to sleep with you."

He stopped trying to kiss me, but then said, "I'm a little excited, do you mind if I relieve myself?"

I was completely taken aback. This was a first. Unsure what to do, I ducked into the bathroom, mumbling that he could use the bathroom to do what he needed to do after I was done.

When I came out of the bathroom, I found him in my kitchen, buck naked, masturbating intensely. I guess he couldn't wait for the bathroom. Thank God he was quick. Then he grabbed some tissues and cleaned everything up. He was actually quite neat.

When he was done, I told him he had to leave. Weirder still—he turned to me, said he had a great time and asked if we could get together again.

- Liza, San Diego, California

Future Dad

On our fifth date I proposed to my husband. We had worked together for several months, so I knew that he was unbelievably funny, kind, honest, and honorable. We were sitting in a restaurant, and he looked deep into my eyes and asked me what I was thinking. I was caught off guard, and replied honestly, "I don't want to frighten you, but I'm thinking that one of these days I'm going to have your children."

Most men are so commitment phobic that I panicked as soon as the words were out. But he replied, "That doesn't frighten me at all—that's the most beautiful thing you could say to me." I learned that not only was he funny and kind, but he was also *brave*. From that moment forward we assumed we would get married, and we both agree that it was the best decision we ever made.

- Mary Ann, Salt Lake City, Utah

L O S E R

Tick Tock Goes the Biological Clock

I met Jeff at a bar one night when I was out with the girls. He was fairly attractive in a Billy Joel sort of way. He was very polite and offered to buy me a drink. We had some nice conversation—enough that I thought I'd like to see him again—and at the end of the evening he asked for my phone number.

That week he asked me to dinner. When he picked me up, he presented me with a red rose. I was delighted! We had a fabulous dinner at a local Italian restaurant. His friend was the chef/owner, so we enjoyed the best table in the house, a very special bottle of wine, and a terrific dinner. All seemed to be going really well until our coffee came. I don't know if he had too much wine or what, but suddenly, in one swift movement, he pushed his chair back, threw his leg up on the table, grabbed a toothpick and shoved it in his mouth and starting sucking on it hard. Then he leaned back, started scratching his chest and demanded, "So how old are you, anyway?"

When I told him I was 27, he said, "Well, you're not getting any younger. You're gonna need to start thinking about having kids soon. If I were you, I'd back off of that career of yours and start seriously thinking about marriage!"

That was our first and last date.

- Michelle, Brick, New Jersey

When I'm Old and Gray . . .

My husband and I started dating in high school. The summer after our junior year Paul had an internship at a hospital where his aunt worked. One night, he came home and told me about an elderly man who had been checked into the hospital. Apparently his grandchildren had shown up at his apartment and found him in a terrible state. He was covered in sores and wearing dirty clothes. As an orderly, the first thing Paul had to do was clean him from head to toe. The gentleman was really suffering from neglect.

I was horrified. I said, "My God, I hope that never happens to me when I get old."

Paul looked at me and said, "The only way that could ever happen to you is if I had been dead a long, long time."

- Lena, Park Slope, New York

LOSER

Fat Chance

Ben and I had been dating for about six months. He was a big teddy bear of a guy from Africa. It wasn't a casual thing. I'd met his family at Christmas—his sisters, everybody. And the sex was amazing. Then suddenly, out of the blue—after having sex, mind you—he told me that he wasn't attracted to me anymore because I was "*way* too fat." I have to say I was very proud of my reaction. Rather than being totally devastated, I said, "Fine, go find yourself a Barbie doll." And I threw him out the door.

- Bronwyn, New York, New York

KEEPER

He Always Keeps Me in Sight

Jason and I had been dating for a few months when we met up after work at a party. Going home, we had two cars. "I'll see you back at my place," he said. It was dark, and I didn't know how to get to his apartment from where we were. I started stressing. *He's going to pull out in front of me, cars will get between us, and I'll never make it back to his apartment.* That's *exactly* what my ex-husband used to do. It was a constant battle with him. He would refuse to give me directions, saying, "Just follow me." Then we'd get on the highway, he'd drive eighty miles an hour, and, since I didn't like to go past the speed limit, I'd lose him and eventually wind up calling him on his cell phone. I'd ask, "Where are you?" And he still wouldn't be very helpful.

That's why I was so impressed with Jason. After he pulled out in front of me, a few cars did get in the way. He actually pulled off to the side of the road to wait for me so I wouldn't get lost. I figured that was a one-time thing, but he pulled over three times before we made it back to his place. He sped up if I needed him to, and slowed down if I needed that. He always kept me in his sight. I thought, *This guy will never leave me behind*. I totally liked that.

- Sandra, South Orange, New Jersey

LOSER

Weathering Heights

Sam took me to the revolving restaurant at the top of the Biltmore Hotel in Los Angeles for a romantic evening. It was our first date, and dinner was lovely. The problems started when it came time to leave. To get down to the street level we could either take the elevator or the escalator. I'm afraid of heights and get nervous going down escalators, so I wanted to take the elevator. But for whatever reason, Sam refused to take the elevator with me. He kept pulling at me to get on the escalator. Finally I said, "Please, I'll meet you out in front of the hotel."

But by the time I got down to street level, he'd left. *He actually left me at the hotel.* I had to borrow money from the bellhop because I had no cash for a taxi. He never called to find out if I made it home, and I didn't feel he was even worth calling to ask what his problem was.

- Ellen, Playa del Rey, California

KEEPER

A Story Woody Allen Would Love!

Thomas and I met on a blind date. As we were getting to know each other he casually mentioned that he had been in transactional analysis therapy. I said, "Oh really, I just made an appointment to see a TA therapist recommended by my friend Jill." When he asked me who, it turned out we were going to the very same therapist. We both laughed. With *all* the therapists in the world we happened to use the same one! (It was like a very bad version of the line in *Casablanca*.) We seemed to be "on the same page"—we had a lot in common.

The next morning I called Jill and asked her if she would mind calling the therapist about Thomas. I really felt comfortable with him and wanted to know what the therapist thought of him. I was just coming off a long, very bad relationship and was very nervous about getting involved again. When Jill asked the therapist, she immediately said, "Oh, Thomas is a wonderful guy. He's so evolved in the group he's almost like an assistant."

I thought, *What could be better than the stamp of approval from a mental health professional!* After we started dating for a while we both went to the therapist to work out any kinks before getting married. The therapist even came and danced at our wedding.

- Maddy, Rockport, Maine

LOSER

A Story Woody Allen Would Film!

A co-worker discovered that the man I'd been dating for about two months was married. Stunned, I called him at home in the evening, and sure enough, a woman answered. I asked for him, and when he came on the line, he sounded flustered.

"David, is there something you want to tell me?"

"I don't know what you mean," he stammered.

"Isn't there something you think maybe I ought to know?"

"You mean about the woman who answered the phone?"

"Yeah!" I said sarcastically. "About *her*."

He claimed they married when they were young, that it didn't work out, and that they were just housemates, free to date others. They'd just recently legalized the breakup.

I didn't buy that, but he insisted on meeting me to talk. I figured one drink wouldn't hurt, and frankly I was looking forward to seeing him try to weasel his way out of this one. We met and he told me I was overreacting, no doubt because of my relationship with my father. He then launched into a discussion about Freud, while I tried to steer the conversation back on topic.

"You don't want to talk about Freud because you don't know anything about Freud!" he countered.

"I know something about Freud," I answered, a Phi Beta Kappa myself. "But this isn't about Freud. It's about you, me, and your *wife*!"

"Face it," he smirked. "I'm just smarter than you."

- Karla, Knoxville, Tennessee

I Have Always Known Him

Hal and I met in Greece one summer at a club. I was just 21 and going into my final year at McGill University in Canada. I was traveling through Europe with some friends. He was 25 and a teacher. I think it was his piercing blue eyes that made him stand out against the crowd. I'd gone to the club with another guy, but I just thought Hal was so handsome that I made sure I got to meet him.

When we first got together, we laughed a lot. I wasn't always comfortable around men, but I was totally comfortable around him. I just had this feeling that I had known him all my life, even though he was brand new to me. (It's not like I'm a New Age kind of person or into crystals or anything like that, but somehow I felt I had known Hal before.) I knew I wanted to see him again.

So I asked him where he was going after Greece. He said he wasn't sure of his itinerary, but he knew he would be in Amsterdam on August 13. I thought fast—I actually had no plans to go to Amsterdam—but I said, "You're kidding? I'm going to be there too! Let's meet."

I enjoyed Israel, my next stop, and then went to Amsterdam on August 13 to meet Hal in front of American Express. He was right on time. We spent the week together. I did run out of money, and he took care of me. (We've been married thirty-one years and have two kids, and he still reminds me of *that*.) I did finally 'fess up that I had no plans to be in Amsterdam, but by that time we were about to celebrate our first anniversary!

- Margo, Toronto, Canada

LOSER

We Won't Always Have Paris

My (now ex-) husband, Will, and I had gone to Paris on vacation to celebrate our anniversary. We'd been partying at a nightclub, and he'd had too much to drink. As we walked back to our hotel, we got into a fierce argument. It was over nothing, really—I hadn't liked the club and was trying to explain why. It was stupid. I mean, who cared? We'd left the club, we weren't going back. I was just expressing my opinion. It was a trifle but, magnified by the alcohol, it got blown all out of proportion, and he was jumping all over me as if my not liking the club was a character flaw. He was so furious that in the middle of the fight he stalked off, leaving me on a corner where we'd stopped to duke it out.

Will has an excellent sense of direction and knew exactly where our hotel was. But I didn't have a clue how to get back. Since I don't speak French, I couldn't even ask for directions. Plus I had no money for a cab. Will was several blocks away before I realized that he wasn't coming back or even waiting for me to catch up to him. If I hadn't chased after him, he would have left me on the street corner.

- Ilene, Hollywood, Florida

KEEPER

Are You a Man or a . . . ?

I knew I was going to keep my boyfriend when I called him at work one night crying because I had just seen a mouse. I was standing up on a chair (like in those cartoons). I refused to move. I just stayed frozen until he got there thirty minutes later. He looked for the mouse but couldn't find it. He stayed with me until I told him he could go back to work. I knew then that if a man was willing to leave his job to come to my apartment to catch a mouse, then he would do just about anything for me. He is very caring, protective, and loving.

- Thelma, Philadelphia, Pennsylvania

LOSER

Feng Hooey

My rock 'n' roll poet boyfriend complained that all of his *chi* was trapped in his penis, giving him chronic pain. He swore the only way he could release the *chi* was to have sex with prostitutes.

- Jo-Lin, Boston, Massachusetts

KEEPER

The Write Stuff

I was 21 and living with my parents after college to save money when I met Craig in a bar one sizzling July night. He was leaving ten days later on his final tour with the Marines—a year-long assignment in Japan. We just clicked. I had a feeling he was the one, but his letters confirmed it.

From the start he was a faithful pen pal. Each week glorious, handwritten letters would arrive on delicate Japanese parchment paper. He was a beautiful writer—sensitive, honest, and with a gift for telling stories of life overseas. Remember, this was a Marine. Yet he was emotional and revealing in his letters. I really got to know him. He managed to call a few times, but it was the letters that I treasured most.

We dated exclusively when he got back. I even took the letters in my suitcase as I packed for our honeymoon. Today they are tucked into a folder in my bedroom armoire. I've taken them out occasionally—anniversaries, nights alone, or while nursing my infant son. I hope my son has inherited his daddy's gift for words.

- Lilly, Cleveland, Ohio

LOSER

Fear Factor

Colin and I had practically grown up together. His father was my elementary school principal, his mother was my Girl Scout troop leader. One summer, I dated one of his friends; another summer he'd dated one of mine. We even had a fling of our own while working summer jobs at a bar in Rhode Island. Our relationship always felt very comfortable. Even though we lived in different cities and were involved in other relationships, we managed to stay connected.

Fast forward about twelve years. Colin was living in New York City. I had a business in Providence, Rhode Island. Every summer he'd ask me to come sailing. It became a joke—I'd promise to go but never would. Finally, I agreed to sail with him to Block Island. I didn't think it was a "date." There were three boats in the party and a ton of people. I was in the back of our boat, and he was at the bow. Suddenly everything came into focus, and I thought, *That's the man. This is where I'm supposed to be.*

The next six months were great. We talked about marriage, the future, buying a summer house on Block Island.

I decided to close my business and move to New York City. I didn't do it for Colin, but he was a factor, and I thought it was great timing. I was embarking on a whole new chapter of my life. I'd worked like crazy to build a business for eight years and didn't have a social life. Now all of a sudden things seemed to be coming together.

But the day I told Colin I was moving to New York City, everything fell apart. From that point on it was never the same relationship. I moved anyway, thinking it would work itself out. It took me a year to figure out that for Colin our relationship was a Great Idea, but when it came down to actually making a decision, he was scared.

- Chloe, New York, New York

Meet the Parents!

I had been dating Nathan for about six months, and he still hadn't met most of my extended family when we decided to visit them in Maine for Passover. We arrived lateish, and everyone else was already there. We walked in, and there was what looked like a receiving line of at least twenty people. I froze. My four brothers were there with assorted wives and kids and girlfriends. As I introduced Nathan down the line, we could hear people talking about him as if he wasn't there. It was like an entire collection of yentas in one room.

I brought him to the kitchen to meet my oldest brother, a real character, who was carving the turkey. He greeted Nathan by pointing this huge carving knife at him. Nathan absolutely rose to the occasion. He was so cute. He had insisted on wearing a shirt and tie, even though I warned him my family was super casual. They even teased him about his outfit. We left the kitchen and the receiving line, and I had no idea how he was reacting. We both looked at each other and burst out laughing.

Nathan looked good on paper—Jewish, nice family, good job. But he was even *better* in person.

- Kim, Bethesda, Maryland

LOSER

Not Quite Kosher

I fell hard for this Jewish guy, David. (I'm Catholic.) He was nice, gentlemanly. He told me he liked my energy—but not in a New Agey sort of way—and that he enjoyed spending time with me. So I was surprised, and felt a little duped, when a few weeks into the relationship he did an about-face and told me he could never get serious with someone who wasn't Jewish.

I suppose there were clues. He wasn't big on shellfish; he'd never call on a Friday night; and the kicker—his father was a rabbi. But since I'd never dated anyone Jewish, I didn't pick up on them. His excuse when I accused him of leading me on was that I should have known when he told me that his father was a rabbi that we were in a "just for fun" relationship. But to my mind, it was as if he'd said his father was a minister. No big deal. I asked him how bad it would be if he brought me home to meet the parents. "Bad," he said, "with a capital B."

Even after that he continued to call me. But I put an end to it. "Unless you're considering becoming Catholic," I told him, "don't call me again."

I mean, what was the point?

- Kathleen, Brooklyn, New York

KEEPER

Ringing in the New Year

Vincent was one of my instructors at the Police Academy, so we'd known each other for years when we started dating. For New Year's Eve 1997 I was on "detail," meaning you go in uniform to a big event. Well, New Year's Eve in Times Square is about as big as it gets. They were expecting about a million people.

I knew it was going to be cold. Vincent helped me dress for the evening—he even lent me a sweater to go over my own bulletproof vest. He asked me to give him a call when I knew where I would be. It was about 8 PM when I called him. "I'm at the corner of Forty-Seventh Street and Eighth Avenue," I said. "Just me and about 400,000 other people." I told him I'd see him later. It was about 11 degrees with a windchill factor of about zero as we were setting up wooden barriers.

He found me a few hours later. Using his influence he "tinned"—flashed his badge—through the barriers in Times Square. Then he tracked down the detail supervisor and asked where I was. He had a big thermos of hot chicken noodle soup and an extra pair of gloves. He stayed with me, and at the stroke of midnight he just planted a kiss on my lips in front of one million people—including all those other cops!

P.S. I have a picture of it.

- Sherry, Queens, New York

LOSER

Should Auld Acquaintance Be Forgot?

My boyfriend invited me to spend New Year's Eve with him in London. At the time he was working in Russia, and I was doing my residency at a hospital in Berlin. It's not easy to get vacation time when you're a resident, but I managed it and booked a flight to London and found a hotel. The plan was that we would spend New Year's Eve day at the National Gallery and then go to a party that night.

We met around 11 AM in front of the huge Christmas tree at the entrance to the National Gallery. Our taste in art was different, so I suggested that we go our own ways. I sped off to look at the Pre-Raphaelites. We were to meet back in front of the Christmas tree in an hour. When I returned, he wasn't there.

I started to panic. Then I stopped myself. Maybe he was in the restroom. Or maybe he'd lost track of time and was still wandering the galleries. I started back through the galleries, slowly combing the crowds for him. I couldn't find him.

I went outside, thinking maybe he'd gotten some fresh air and was lingering on the steps. Nothing. I checked with the clerks at the gallery entrance. No one had seen him. There was no message at the information counter. Or at the hotel. He simply vanished.

I spent New Year's Eve by myself. I didn't know anyone in London, and I couldn't leave because I didn't have a flight out until January 1. I was furious. You don't abandon someone in a foreign city. My boyfriend never showed up or called or wrote, so I have never discovered what happened. And I was too embarrassed to call his parents' house. To make things worse, I caught a bad case of bronchitis. I had to call in sick at the hospital, which is not good when you're a resident, and my mother had to come to care for me for a week until I recovered. A bad New Year's Eve. A horrible illness. A minus balance all the way around.

- Agnes, New York, New York

KEEPER

If Music Be the Food of Love, Play On

We had a little bet going this Valentine's Day because we both find the day so overmarketed. The bet was to see who could be the most creative with a gift, but the most we could spend was $10. James always jokes that he expects to win the lottery someday, so I bought him a bunch of lottery tickets and some chocolates.

When it was time for my gift, he said, "I only spent 75 cents on you, but it's going to make you cry."

I opened up the little package and inside was a CD he had burned and labeled, "Time after time, a musical journey of our love affair." The first song was, in fact, the very first song that was playing in my car on our first date. The whole CD was all these meaningful songs that he had put together just for me. He won the bet and my heart all over again.

- Carly, Freehold, New Jersey

LOSER

With Friends Like These . . .

One afternoon while I was doing laps at the gym, this guy Peter approached me in the pool. We'd both come up for air, and he commented that I was a strong swimmer. We started chatting, and—I remember it was Valentine's Day—he asked if I had a sweetheart. When I said no, he said he'd like to take me out.

The day of our date he called me to say he was going to be late and asked if I'd meet him at his place. I thought that was strange for a first date, but I'm a good sport so I bought some wine and headed over.

When Peter was ready to go, he mentioned that he wasn't really feeling well. He thought he caught a cold from his pet ferret (the same one that he insisted on introducing me to). While I'm thinking, *Should I run?* Peter added that his roommate Doug wanted to come along on our date. Already this was shaping up into a winner of a night. I suggested that we go to a nearby sports bar where friends of mine were sure to be hanging out, so it wouldn't be just the three of us.

The evening grew still weirder. I ended up paying for my own dinner—Peter didn't even offer. Then, driving home he was so tired from not feeling well and working a long day that he actually nodded off at the wheel and hit the car in front of us. At that point I'd had enough. After making sure everyone was okay, I started walking home. Doug offered to walk me. All I could think of was that this was the strangest date I'd ever been on.

The next day Doug came over and asked my doorman to ring my apartment so he could invite me to lunch. "Listen," I said through the intercom. "You're nice, but you're Peter's roommate, so no thank you. I'm not interested."

No sooner had I finished with Doug, when Peter called to ask me out again. I said, "Your roommate was just here asking me out. You guys should get your act together. And by the way, I'm not interested in either of you."

- Sheila, New York, New York

KEEPER

Valentine's Every Day

My husband is not romantic in the traditional sense. He is apt to forget birthdays and anniversaries and whiz right past Valentine's Day with nary a card or present. When we were first married, I used to get angry and hurt about his casual attitude about what I thought he was supposed to do, even though I knew from the start that he has a basically rebellious, up-yours nature. But over time it came to me that actually he is *always* giving me gifts, coming home all year round with stuff he knows that I would enjoy or that would cheer me up or make me laugh or help me through a particular problem.

He's walked a mile for the Sunday *New York Times* in a blizzard because he knows what a pleasure it is for me to spend hours with it. I didn't ask him to; he went out to get the paper as usual. It just wouldn't have occurred to him to come home without it.

We've rented houses on the shore because I'm partial to the ocean, although he really prefers the countryside and mountains. So he ignores Valentine's Day. Big deal. He gives me a Valentine every single day.

- Alice, Columbus, Ohio

LOSER

Open Card, Insert Foot

A friend introduced me to a guy friend of hers who had transferred to the same university I was going to. We were total opposites. He was a Republican. I was more liberal. He was in finance. I was interested in art. Even so, we got along well. And we *really* connected sexually. After a while, I thought, *Well, maybe opposites do attract*. I was starting to think that maybe, after all, he was The One.

Then he sent me a Valentine's Day card. Inside, he wrote, "For someone who didn't attend the School of Finance, you're pretty smart."

I'm not sure how the words "School of Finance" get into a Valentine's Day card, but I wasn't hanging around to find out.

- Brenda, Dallas, Texas

KEEPER

Sexy Tool Lady

I told my boyfriend that this year I had a very short wish list for my birthday. What I wanted most was a tool kit—whenever I needed to fix something minor, I would find the kids had raided the toolbox and it was a real mess. I wanted my very own tools. So I opened up my present, and there was the tool kit. Then I noticed there was another envelope. I opened it, and laughed out loud. It was a gift certificate to Victoria's Secret. Pierre insisted, "If you give a lady a tool kit, she should be a *sexy* lady."

- Patricia, Raleigh, South Carolina

LOSER

Gangsta Love

I'm drawn to artists, writers, educators, and creative people. But since I was still unattached, my friends would tell me, "Not everyone can be an intellectual. Men can have other qualities that are just as valuable." And my personal favorite, "Get off your high horse, and broaden your field of who you consider eligible."

So it was with this new attitude that I found myself at a country western bar outside of Boston one night, dancing with a Rocky lookalike. Frank was a contractor. I could tell immediately that he wasn't well educated, but he seemed like an okay guy. He asked if he could take me out, and I thought, *What the hell? Why not?*

Frank picked me up in a black Cadillac. He was wearing a three-piece suit. He was very courteous, and he certainly wasn't cheap. During dinner he ordered up a storm and kept asking me if I wanted anything else, did I want to have some of this and taste some of that? He was trying to dazzle me. And I was swept away by his effort. After dinner he took me dancing. We had a lot of fun. I went out with him one other night, and we also had a great time. Then I didn't hear from him again.

Two months later he called me, saying, "I'm really sorry you haven't heard from me, but I've been in the slammer."

The slammer? Who talks like that? I'd never heard that as any excuse for a guy not calling. It was so off the wall, it had to be true.

He told me that he had been with a client in a dangerous neighborhood in Boston when a gang member grabbed the client and put a knife to his throat. Frank pulled out a Magnum .44. (I didn't even know he carried a gun.) He told the kid to drop the knife or he'd shoot. The kid refused and so he shot him—thankfully just wounding him in the leg. But he'd spent two months in jail. So he was just out of the slammer and had gone home to shower. Now he was calling me. This was just a little too much drama. I figured I couldn't handle someone who carried around a Magnum .44.

Celia, Framingham, Massachusetts

He Came Gift Wrapped

When I met Marcus I wasn't looking for a boyfriend. I was preoccupied with my mother who had just had surgery. I was trying to get ready for a trip to see her and the rest of my family for Christmas. I wanted to see him too, but I was rushed and didn't have enough time to prepare for the holiday. When Marcus came over to my apartment, I had a really big pile of gifts for my six brothers and sisters and friends that still needed to be wrapped.

He said, "Why don't I help you wrap them?"

I remember thinking, *Could he really be saying that?*

He sat down and started to wrap the gifts. At first I just watched him. He's an engineer. He was meticulous. He was measuring ribbon and folding perfectly and lining the paper up just right. He helped me wrap every single gift for my family whom he had never even met. And this was just the second date. I knew he was special.

- Caren, Washington, DC

LOSER

No Littering

My boyfriend Bart came to visit me in Seattle. I'd been having second thoughts and wasn't sure that I felt the same way about him, so as it was, I was lukewarm about his visit. I was still going to be at work when he arrived, so I told him just to let himself into my apartment and wait for me.

When I got home, I was no longer undecided—we were definitely breaking up. As I walked in, I found the entire kitchen floor covered in beer cans. He was hanging out, guzzling beer, tossing the cans on the floor as he finished them. There was a whole case of empty beer cans scattered all over my floor.

Bart didn't see anything wrong with it. What was strange was that I'd known him for years, and his apartment was spotless. I was so digusted, I asked him to leave. But because there weren't any flights out that day, he ended up back at my apartment four hours later, even more drunk. That night I let him sleep on the couch. The next morning, I woke him up and tossed him out for good. I cleaned up the beer cans myself.

- Elizabeth, Seattle, Washington

KEEPER

He's Head and Shoulders above the Rest

As a freelance writer I'm usually in my office, interviewing experts, phone cradled on my shoulder typing their comments into my computer as fast as I can. And I'm often complaining out loud about my sore neck!

Not long ago my husband came home from work and dropped a Radio Shack box on my desk. (I'm very low-tech and never browse through electronics stores or catalogs.) Inside was a good-quality headset telephone. "I couldn't stand to see you contorting yourself anymore," he told me. Now, of course, I can't imagine how I'd ever manage without my headset—or my thoughtful mate.

- Carolyn, Buffalo, New York

LOSER

A Job Worth Doing . . .

I was dating a guy who worked for his dad and eventually wanted to take over his family's business. He regularly worked sixty to seventy hours a week. At the same time I was working for an Internet company, putting in about fifty to sixty hours a week. But strangely he just couldn't understand my own ambition. He was always prodding, "Why do you work so hard? Just work forty hours. You don't own the company. Why do you care?"

Well, I care because that's who I am. And when I have a job to do, I do it till it's done. I told him, "If you can't live with that, you'll live without me." I could never be with a man who didn't understand my own work ethic.

- Tina, Boston, Massachusetts

KEEPER

My Business Is His Business

My mom will tell anyone who will listen that she knew my guy was a Keeper when he bought me a computer for Christmas, our first as a couple. I wanted to write, and Dave gave me the means to do so. He has since proven his devotion with many surprise vacations and clever gifts, along with his abiding love, respect, and friendship.

But what has proven his Keeper status is his support of my growing career. Being married to a fiction writer is not easy—the hours spent writing, editing, and promoting; the out-of-the-way research trips; vacations scheduled around writing conferences. Not only does he tolerate the craziness of my career, he embraces it. He gladly assumes the role of "Mr. Nina" at conferences, even wearing a badge! He listens, helps me plot, and has made it his business to understand the writing business. And his most recent surprise: he had a website designed for me! Now that's a Keeper.

- Nina, Miami, Florida

LOSER

Stripped Down Party

I'd spent a lot of time planning a Christmas party. I'm an exotic dancer and a lot of my friends are dancers, but I didn't want it to be a stripper party. It was supposed to be a warm, family-type party. But when my boyfriend arrived, he rallied all of my guests to go to the strip club where I worked. When I complained, he said, "Don't be a party pooper."

But it was *Christmas,* and he wanted to take all of my guests to the strip joint where I worked. Hell no, I didn't want to go there that night. After he pulled that stunt, it was over. I was done with him.

- Marnie, Las Vegas, Nevada

What a Doll!

After my husband and I got married we moved from West Virginia to North Carolina. I took most of my stuff from home on the initial move; however, I left my china doll at my mom's house because I didn't want it to get broken. My late grandmother had given it to me when I was seven, the only thing my grandmother had ever given to me personally. She admonished me to "take good care of it."

On one of our return trips for a visit, my mom had this "look" on her face when we walked in the door. She tearfully explained that a picture in my bedroom had somehow fallen off the wall and landed right on my doll, shattering the entire head. I was really upset, and I knew my mom felt just terrible.

Several months later on my birthday, my husband presented me with this beautifully wrapped present. I couldn't imagine what it was, because he usually asks for hints about what I want. When I opened that box, I just started crying. It was my doll. He had painstakingly glued all those small broken pieces back together!

He said he knew how much the doll meant to me, and he wanted me to have it back, even if it wasn't perfect anymore. I told him it was even more perfect because of his thoughtfulness.

- Chloe, Insurance, West Virginia

LOSER

Put Your Two Cents In

My boyfriend was unbelievably stingy. When I lived in his house, I had to pay him *in cash* for half the rent and half the utilities, and I had to do all of the dishes and clean the house as my "keep" for staying there. Every time we went out, I paid half. Even when I was unemployed, I still had to pay my half—down to the penny. One night we got into a fight in a restaurant over—get this—two cents. I owed him two more pennies, and I didn't have them in my wallet. This from a man who makes $125,000 a year.

I finally got fed up when my grandfather died. I didn't have enough money to buy a plane ticket to go to Shreveport, Louisiana, for the funeral. My boyfriend offered to loan me the money—at 8 percent interest! It took me three months to pay him back. He didn't even give me a ride to the airport. I had to take a cab.

- Joan, Denver, Colorado

KEEPER

Just the Fax, Ma'am

When my daughter needed surgery, our HMO gave me a hard time. I knew there would be several forms that I would have to fax over to the HMO, but I didn't have a fax at home or at the school where I taught. I had just started dating Jeffrey, and I asked him if he'd take the forms to his office and fax them out if I needed him to. Sure enough, the following day I needed the forms faxed. I called Jeffrey at work, and he promptly sent them out.

When he came to pick me up for our date that weekend, he handed me a box with a brand-new fax machine. He said, "No one should be left without a fax machine."

- Rae, Bangor, Maine

LOSER

Dollar Bill Bob

Back in college, I'd met this guy named Bob at a St. Patrick's Day parade. We exchanged numbers and set a date to go hear a band at a nearby club. Since I spent my weekends at my parents' house, he picked me up, came in, and met them. So far, so good.

But as we were driving to the club, he said, "I just want to tell you I only have a dollar on me. Do you have any money?"

"Are you kidding me?" This was our first date. "You have *no* money on you? You couldn't even borrow any money?"

"Nah," he said. "I was hoping you'd have money."

We were supposed to be meeting another friend of mine at the club. Otherwise I would have made him turn around and take me home. I was so mad. I didn't talk to him on the drive down and when we got to the club, I just hung out with my girlfriend and ignored him for the rest of the night. Now when we talk about him, we call him Dollar Bill Bob.

Siobhan, Hazlet, New Jersey

Picture Me Happy

There's a local artist here in Bermuda whose work I'm excited about. I loved the illustrations she had originally done for a book, and the original drawings were now on sale. I had a feeling my husband, Patrick, might buy me a specific illustration I had admired. When he told me he already got me my Christmas gift, I said, "Patrick, I hope you didn't buy me that picture." I loved it, but it was $5,000!

On Christmas morning I saw this huge package shaped like a painting. I was excited, but I really wished he hadn't spent that much money. However, when I unwrapped it, it wasn't the picture I expected. It was a portrait of one of my students done by the same artist. Patrick had picked the student he thought was my favorite, then arranged a portrait sitting through the child's grandmother. The artist took a photograph and then did the painting. But when I look at the painting, I don't just see that one student. It's *every* child I've ever worked with. He just has that look on his face that says, "I get it!" It's the look that makes every teacher glad she teaches. It was a fabulous gift.

P.S. On Valentine's Day Patrick gave me the picture I said I didn't want, but really did! So now I have two works done by this fabulous artist.

- Alicia, Hamilton, Bermuda

LOSER

Taxed to the Max

Things hadn't been going well in my marriage for a long time, but I kept pretending everything was okay because I had this Calvinist you-make-your-bed-now-lay-in-it upbringing. So I just made excuses for Bruce and lived my own life independently.

But the final straw came when I was doing our taxes. Bruce had a salaried position, so his taxes were automatically taken out of his paycheck. For five years I had been filling out the forms. He had been telling me that he was mailing them in. But he never filed the paperwork. Actually, he was just putting them into his coat pocket. One day I was cleaning out our closet and I discovered all of our tax forms dating back to the year we married, neatly folded in their envelopes, all stamped and ready to go. I was horrified when I realized his deception . . . and the hefty penalties we were facing. I finally got a lawyer and left.

- Jennifer, New York, New York

KEEPER

The Night the Lights Went Out . . .

We experienced a major blackout in the summer of 1973 in New York City. That night all the traffic lights were out, and there was a lot of looting. It was like a bad sci-fi movie, with windows breaking all over the city.

I was working as a nurse in the intensive care unit at a major medical center. I had the evening shift, when the blackout hit at 9:10 PM. About twenty seconds later, the emergency backup lights kicked in. About thirty seconds after that, the nursing supervisor called to make sure we were okay. I was in charge and assured her that we were fine. Right after I hung up with my supervisor the phone rang again. It was my boyfriend. "Hi. I'm on my way to pick you up," he said. "I hear it's going to be dangerous out there." That was the entire conversation. He just got in the car and came to get me.

No other boyfriend or husband showed up that night, and most of the other women didn't even leave the hospital until the next day.

- Barbara, Queens, New York

LOSER

Do-It-Yourself Sex

On our third date Ron brought me a box of Godiva chocolates that was like a pirate chest, full of gold doubloons. Underneath the candies he'd hidden a bunch of gold coin condoms. I thought that was cute—and promising. And in fact, when we got into bed, I was like, *Whoo hoo!* He had the biggest equipment I'd ever seen. Unfortunately, he didn't have a clue how to use it. Sex with him was never fantastic . . . or even satisfying. But worst of all, one night he finished, and I hadn't. He looked me straight in the eye and said, "I'm done. If you're not, do it yourself."

Sacha, Chicago, Illinois

Some Keepers Are Made, Not Born!

When it comes to giving gifts and learning how to celebrate, my husband didn't start off as a Keeper. He would often just run out on his lunch hour to get something, and for our first Valentine's Day, he gave me a beautiful gold locket inscribed, "To Sally, from Ted."

"What happened to the 'love'?" I said.

"Well, my father picked it out and had it engraved," he answered.

I told him, "I should be getting it from you, not your father. If you get me a gift, you have to think about it, pick it out, buy it with care, and afterward write something nice on the card. You see the way I buy *you* gifts. It takes weeks. If I buy you a sweater, it has to be the right color, the right size. It has to be beautiful and perfect for you."

I started to train him because I knew he meant well. And over thirty-five years he really listened.

I recently celebrated my sixtieth birthday. When I said I didn't want a party, he was the one who said, "You have to celebrate this the right way. Whether we can afford it or not, you are having a party." I wound up having a wonderful party.

This Mother's Day, I wasn't expecting anything. That's when he really surprised me. He had seen me looking at a Fortunoff's catalogue. He picked out a gorgeous pin and left it for me on my pillow. I was shocked.

He said, "This is for you, because I know you'll love it."

Sure enough, I love it—and I love him. He was always sweet, but clueless about gifts. Not anymore.

- Sally, Westchester, New York

LOSER

Sofa, So Bad

Back in college, a guy I was dating told me he'd given me crabs. He tried to convince me that he'd gotten them from his *sofa*. Naturally, I didn't buy it. I was so disgusted. I shudder to think where he did get them from—not his sofa, though perhaps from whom he was on the sofa with!

- Janine, Durham, North Carolina

KEEPER

He Threw in the Towel!

I've received many gifts from the men I've dated over the years—jewelry, clothing, once even a trip to Europe. But the one that touched me the most was a set of plush white bath towels that my partner gave me in the beginning of our relationship when I started spending a lot of time at his place. He lives a bachelor's life in a remote part of the Southwest with few creature comforts. The bath towels showed me that taking care of me was a high priority for him, and he was thinking about what would make me more comfortable. (And most important, that he expected me to be around in his life.) He has since bought me flowers for Valentine's Day, a Palm Pilot for Christmas, and expensive jewelry. But I smile every time I think about those bath towels.

- Sonya, Jean, Nevada

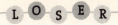

The Gift That Keeps on Giving

I was working as a lifeguard at the pool in an apartment complex. Paul was the boiler room operator. He used to come down to the pool around sunset when it would be quiet, and we'd hang out. I was about 19; he was older, probably around 26. At the time I thought he was warm, sweet, and sophisticated. And it was really exciting—here was this responsible adult interested in *me*. Plus, the sex was great. I was enthralled with him.

With all that great sex, he gave me genital warts. My gynecologist found them during a routine visit. I remember calling Paul and telling him that he'd given me these warts, and him denying the whole thing. He never took responsibility for it or admitted that he gave them to me. I'd been crazy for him, and I paid for it. I had to have the warts burned off six times over the next six to eight months because they kept coming back. The warts lasted longer than the relationship did.

- Courtney, Manahawkin, New Jersey

KEEPER

Brilliant Minds Think Alike

It was our eleventh anniversary, not exactly a major event. I decided to buy Brad an automatic coffee maker we had seen at Zabar's—a fancy supermarket on the Upper West Side in Manhattan. I liked the idea that it could turn itself on so we could stay in bed late on Sunday mornings. When Brad opened the gift, he burst out laughing. I couldn't figure out why until I opened *my* gift. He'd bought me the same exact coffee maker. The only issue was which of them to return—we had even bought them in the same color.

- Rachel, Ann Arbor, Michigan

LOSER

Can You Hear Me Now?

I was dating a guy who was super nice, but we didn't always connect in conversation. I'd talk, and he'd zone out or say weird things that indicated he wasn't on the same wavelength with me. I tried to tell him that I didn't feel like we were communicating. He was sweet, but he didn't get it. I finally gave up one night after we were driving home from my parents' house. I was trying to tell him about some heart-wrenching thing my mother had done that upset me. I was giving him all of the background. We were at the climactic part of the story when I paused and said, "And then you know what happened . . ."

Just then we passed a bakery, and he said, "Hey, that bakery is open on Sundays."

I just couldn't believe it. "This is like a sitcom," I said. "Do you hear yourself?"

"What?" he seemed surprised. "I'm listening."

Yeah, right.

- Kristin, Hartford, Connecticut

KEEPER

Happy Birthday to You . . .

I was about to turn 60, and rather than have a party Nick and I decided to go to Italy. But he knew me well enough to know that in my heart of hearts I didn't want my birthday to go unacknowledged. Since there wasn't an actual event attached to it, I had no easy way of letting people know.

Nick made sure that my friends didn't overlook the day. He called a few key people in my life and told them to tell others so I would get lots of cards. I got more than thirty. I didn't catch on right away when they started arriving, but afterward he told me that since, in some cases, he was contacting old friends who I hadn't talked to in quite a while, he ended up having long catch-up conversations on the phone. That slowed him down. So he didn't even have a chance to contact everyone on his list.

On the actual day of my birthday, he plastered our living room walls and tabletops with framed photos of me at various joyful moments of my life: my Sweet 16 party, a costume Halloween party with Nick in our late twenties, finishing my first mini marathon in my thirties, vacationing with our daughter Elise at the beach in my forties, a trip to Europe in my fifties. The cards and the photos formed a scrapbook of my life, our life together.

- Barbara, New York, New York

LOSER

Birthday Blues

I was sure that my college boyfriend and I would break up when he moved to San Francisco to take a new job. But he missed me and flew back to New York City to ask me to marry him. He was still living in San Francisco, and we were planning the wedding and trying to find a place to live. For about six months everything was fine, until I went to visit him for my thirtieth birthday.

The first clue something was wrong was that he didn't pick me up at the airport. Then on my birthday, not only didn't he take the day off to be with me after I'd traveled to see him, but he worked until 8 PM. On his way home he picked up a coffee percolator from Williams-Sonoma as my birthday gift. He gave it to me in the Williams-Sonoma bag. I don't even think there was a card.

At first I tried to pass it off that he was under a lot of pressure with a new job and being in a new city. But when you're engaged to be married, and you're really together, then you do special things. You get excited that your fiancée is coming to visit on her thirtieth birthday, you get a thoughtful gift, and you make special plans. His actions were speaking louder than his words. We'd known each other for twelve years, and I realized that he couldn't talk to me about whether he was having reservations about getting married. I didn't want to marry him if he couldn't deal with what was really going on, so I called off the engagement.

- Terri, New York, New York

KEEPER

Oh, You *Should* Have . . .

I showed my husband, Steve, the new green leather pants I bought at a fancy boutique in our neighborhood. He knew this was a real splurge for me—I had just lost a lot of weight and wanted to show off my new backside. I happened to mention to him that the pants had a matching jacket but I hadn't wanted to spend the money on it. I totally forgot about that conversation until about a week later. I opened up my closet and there was the jacket hanging over the pants. Steve hates to go shopping, so it really meant a lot to me. (He confided later he couldn't believe how long it took me to discover the jacket!)

- Sarah, San Francisco, California

LOSER

Cheap Trick

I was dating a professor who was notoriously cheap. But he was also witty, super smart, charming, and fun, so we continued to date. That is, until the car theft incident.

We had driven from Washington, DC, to New York City to see a concert. Afterward, we were to stay at the professor's brother's apartment. Our bags were in the trunk. I packed my hippest out-on-the-town clothes; he had some old clothes and a few papers that needed grading. I begged him to drop the luggage at his brother's before the show, but he insisted on going straight to the concert and there was no way to get him to spring for a parking spot in a garage.

The thieves took everything—even his students' papers. We filed a police report, I cataloged my $1,000 worth of lost goods (my Neiman Marcus boots were brand new), and we went home the next morning. He didn't bother to tally up a figure for his items because even the Salvation Army wouldn't take his old clothes.

A few months later, he casually mentioned that he'd gotten "a few hundred dollars" from the insurance company for the stolen items. When I asked about my share, he looked at me blankly, then muttered something about having bought CDs with the cash.

- Lynne, Washington, DC

KEEPER

He Always Trusted My Judgment

When my boys were young, maybe 3 and 5, I went to get tickets for a local appearance of their favorite group—The Three Stooges. When I returned home, my husband called and asked where I had been when he called earlier. Jokingly I said, "I was out shopping and purchased a complete set of furniture for the living room." Believe me, we had no extra money for me to be out furniture shopping.

"How come you didn't tell me you were going shopping?" he asked.

"Sorry, it was a spontaneous decision."

That was the end of the conversation.

That evening I told my mother, who was visiting. She said, "Milt is too good to be believed." She was determined to get a rise out of him over dinner. When Milt asked me to tell him more about the furniture I bought, I didn't get a chance to say anything, because my mother interrupted and said very dramatically that I had "frivolously spent our entire savings on unnecessary furniture" and that she was very disappointed in my judgment. Milton said, "Mom, if that was June's decision, she had to have had a reason. That's good enough for me. But she could have told me she was going shopping."

I was so touched by his faith in me that I started to cry. After wiping away my tears, I told him I had been putting him on, and that I hoped I would never betray his vote of confidence in me.

We just celebrated our fiftieth anniversary. I kept my promise.

- June, Westhampton, New York

LOSER

Money for Nothing

I never minded that Rick was often strapped for cash. But he had a habit of never letting me know that he didn't have enough cash on hand until the bill came. He was forever putting me in situations where eventually somebody could be washing dishes.

One night we'd gone to a birthday dinner at a restaurant. He swore he had enough cash, that it was going to be $50 for each couple. But when the check came, it turned out to be $100 per couple. But even if it had been $50, he still didn't have enough—he'd brought only $48 with him. Another time we were standing on line to buy half-priced tickets to a Broadway show. Again he said he had everything covered. But when we got to the ticket window, he didn't have enough and, once again, I had to lay out money—though this time I walked him to a bank machine so he could pay me back immediately.

I probably could have dealt with this particular habit, except that I discovered he was stealing money—from my mother. I never noticed money missing, but every time Rick was in the house, my mother would come to me a day or two later and say she was missing such and such amount. My mother is meticulous about her money; she balances her checkbook to the penny. Rick was taking money out of her wallet. And it wasn't until a mutual friend mentioned that he had also stolen from her—she used to leave money around as "bait," and it was always missing when he left—that I put it all together. Rick denied it, of course. But after we broke up, he gave our friend $100 to give to me. I guess he felt guilty.

- Manya, Brooklyn, New York

K E E P E R

Wake-Up Call

My boyfriend Fred and I got into the habit of always contacting each other on our cell phones just to say good morning. We both have kids and lead hectic lives, but we manage to sort of wake each other up that way.

On this particular day I had to go to work, but he had the day off. Even so, he remembered to set his alarm to make sure he woke up in time just to make our daily phone call. He didn't want to miss a day.

* Janice, Charlotte, North Carolina

LOSER

Rude Awakening

I was in Aruba on vacation with my girlfriends when I met this guy who owned one of the hotel/casinos. It was one of these whirlwind romances. Every night it was dinner and a show. When I left to go home, he visited me regularly. Pretty soon he persuaded me to give up my job in New York City and move to Aruba with him. Unfortunately, it turned out that I couldn't stand living in Aruba. I'm not an island person. But Gabriel also had a beautiful house in Fort Lauderdale, right on the water, so I moved there. However, because he often traveled for business, Gabriel was hardly ever there. At least I *thought* he wasn't there. One morning he really surprised me.

It was very early when I felt something waking me up. I opened my eyes and looked down at the end of the bed. There was Gabriel, kissing my feet. Only it wasn't just my feet. He had somehow managed to strap on a pair of very hooker-like five-inch heels without disturbing me. He was busily licking the shoes while, ah . . . "pleasuring" himself. It totally grossed me out, but I didn't want him to know he'd woken me up—since he clearly didn't want me awake—so I pretended to still be asleep until he was done. Suddenly I had a very sick feeling that he'd done this before. I'm a pretty sound sleeper, but after this happened, I started to remember other little things that I'd always passed off as weird dreams.

Once he was out of the house, I packed my things and left.

● Kate, New York, New York

KEEPER

Where There's Smoke . . .

My boyfriend Chris wanted to cook me a romantic meal at his apartment. But when I got there I realized he had never, ever used his oven. In fact, when I opened it I noticed Tupperware-like containers in the broiler. Since he couldn't quite figure out how to turn it on, we gave up and ordered pizza.

Later on we were awakened in the middle of the night by the smoke alarm going off. Without missing a beat, Chris pushed me naked out of bed, wrapped me in his robe and tied a belt around it. He got me out of his apartment and on to the street.

Shaking, he came down and joined me. (In fiddling around with the oven, it turns out he'd turned it on. The plastic containers melted, causing the thick smoke.) He hugged me close and said, "All I was worried about was you. Anything in the apartment—they are only things." That's when I knew he wanted to keep me, and I him.

- Bonnie, Willmington, Delaware

LOSER

Jeepers Peepers

I'm a night person, and my boyfriend Dan would often go to bed before me. One hot summer night I was laying naked on the couch watching TV when I heard rustling noises outside. We had shutters on the windows, and at first I thought it was the wind. But I kept hearing this sound. So I went over to the window and checked. There was a guy standing there peering at me through the shutters, with his pants down, jerking off. I freaked out and started screaming. I ran into the bedroom, yelling to Dan, "Call 911! There's a sicko at the window!" But Dan would not wake up. He literally rolled over and went back to sleep. I called 911 myself.

Fortunately my screaming got the attention of my landlord, a parole officer who lived upstairs. He came down. The cops came and searched the area. There was all kinds of commotion. They never did find the peeper. And Dan never once got out of bed to see what was wrong. He didn't even ask me about it the next morning.

- Kimberly, Bronx, New York

KEEPER

For As Long As You Need Me

I was only dating Max for about two months when my company sent me to Germany for a month. I didn't really want to go, and I felt very isolated because I didn't speak the language. By the time I arrived back home, I had really bad stomach pains. When I called the doctor, he said I probably had an ulcer, and he recommended I take some over-the-counter pills.

The medicine didn't help, and when Max came over the next day he saw how much pain I was in. He found my address book and called my doctor, who said I needed to go to the emergency room. Max gathered up my purse and took me to the hospital. He listened to the emergency room doctor's directions because I wasn't able to pay attention. (It turned out I *did* have an ulcer.)

Then Max took me home, went to the pharmacy, and filled the prescription. He stayed with me for the next two days. When I called my best friend, she said, "You went to the hospital and no one called *me*?" You see, my last boyfriend would always call *her* when I didn't feel good. He didn't do well with illness! The way Max took care of me made a huge impression.

- Janie, Los Angeles, California

LOSER

Ill Advised

I'd been window shopping on my way home one night when I noticed a guy from the neighborhood walking behind me. We started talking and seemed to have a lot in common—both of us were into health and fitness. By the time we'd walked home, we'd made a date for dinner.

When he called to confirm our date, I mentioned that I felt like I was getting a cold. He immediately backed out, saying that he couldn't afford to get sick. He got very panicky about the whole situation. I thought he was being really presumptuous, assuming we'd have the kind of physical contact on our first date that would get him sick. If he wanted to get to know me, we could still have gone out—he could have kept his distance so he wouldn't be exposed to my cold. But there was no caring or consciousness about me—it was all about him. When he called back to reschedule, I told him I wasn't interested.

- Clea, Washington, DC

Modern-Day Sir Galahad

I'd woken up with a stomach flu. I felt awful but, workaholic that I was, decided to try to go to work anyway since I had a lunch conference to go to and a desk full of work that needed my attention. I managed to get showered and dressed, but I was so queasy I didn't think I could handle the lurching of the subway, so my boyfriend (who worked in the same office) and I took a cab into the city.

What a mistake! Morning traffic was terrible, and the cabdriver's hitting the brakes as we crept along the highway was doing nothing to calm my jumpy stomach. Sure enough, as we cleared the Brooklyn Bridge I started vomiting. Quick thinker that he is, Ed took off his jacket and held it under my chin so I wouldn't mess up the cab and piss off the driver.

Surely this was a modern-day equivalent of spreading the cloak over the mud for the lady to walk on. The jacket was ruined. But he'd won my heart.

- Jackie, Brooklyn, New York

LOSER

In Health, Not Sickness

Every month I get incapacitating migraines. The pain is so intense even powerful prescription painkillers can't touch it, and all I can do is lay down in a dark room with an ice pack and wait it out.

Even though it's the same every month, and I know that within forty-eight hours or so the migraine will pass, being in that much agony for that long is still scary because I feel so out of control—especially when I can't stop throwing up. That's the worst, slouched over the toilet, not being able to breathe.

Unfortunately my (now ex-) husband was not the most sympathetic caretaker. Since he was rarely ill and wanted to be left alone when he was, he could not understand why I craved so much coddling when I was sick. In fact, he'd often make me feel guilty for even being ill. So there I'd be in the bathroom, retching uncontrollably, and his way of checking on me would be to call out from the living room where he'd be reading or watching TV, "Are you dead yet?"

- Rachelle, Dania, Florida

KEEPER

Workplace Romeo

It was really late, about two in the morning. I was exhausted, but I was stuck in the newsroom working on deadline. At that point my husband and I were still in the "just dating" stage. Fred decided to surprise me by picking me up from work. He snuck into the boss's office and got on the PA system. I could hear this silly name only *he* calls me. He was whispering to me and making kissing noises.

He made sure everyone else had cleared out. (I hope!)

- Rachel, Ames, Iowa

LOSER

Office Oaf

My boyfriend David really wanted to get married and have kids right away. I hadn't dated that much, but I thought I was *supposed* to want to get married and have kids. So after four months of dating, when he asked me to marry him, I said okay. A month later I got cold feet and broke off the engagement. I loved David, I just wasn't sure what I wanted to do.

But the moment of absolute This Isn't Going to Work came while I was working late. My office is very small; everyone can hear everyone else's conversation. David called me, in a panic, screaming, "You gave me VD!"

"What?!" I'm stunned.

David's doctor had diagnosed a throat infection as gonorrhea. "You have to go to the doctor right away!" he screamed.

"What?!" I'm repeating stupidly. I'm thinking, *It's 6:30 PM. The doctor's not open at 6:30 PM.* "Do I need to go to the emergency room or can this wait till tomorrow?" I asked, trying to keep my voice as low as possible.

David acknowledged that it could wait till morning, but he kept saying, "You slept with someone! How else do I have this disease? I didn't sleep with anyone!"

"I'm not saying you slept with anyone," I replied evenly. "I'm saying maybe there's been a mistake." Because he'd started antibiotics, he couldn't be retested. Meanwhile, I was terrified. *What was it?* The next morning I saw my doctor and got tested for *everything*—gonorrhea, AIDS, syphilis.

It turned out everything was fine. I didn't have a sexually transmitted disease at all. Whatever mystery infection David had, it wasn't an STD.

Now it was my turn to be pissed. Not only had David called me screaming, knowing I worked in a small office where everyone could hear every word, but it was clear he didn't trust me. My first thought was that the doctor had erred; his was that I'd slept around.

- Leah, Salem, Massachusetts

KEEPER

Hey, Big Spender!

I was 21 and engaged. My fiancé Tom and I really wanted a big wedding with my best friends as bridesmaids. My parents seemed to go along with that. Then suddenly—at least it seemed that way to me—they announced to Tom and I that they were getting a divorce. I was shocked. My father made it clear that there would be no money for a big wedding so we could just forget about it.

Tom, who was 27 and established in his career as a banker, simply told my dad, "This is *our* wedding, and we can afford to do it right, just the way Beth wants it."

I was so proud of him.

Then he added, "And of course you can come and enjoy yourself."

- Beth, Washington, DC

LOSER

Risky Business

Howard was constantly borrowing money from me. Sometimes he'd pay it back, but then he'd borrow more. It was really aggravating. Evenutally he owed me about $1,000. One day I discovered that the reason he was always in debt to me was that he was losing thousands of dollars playing the options market. I eventually got my money back . . . but I let him go.

- Michelle, Stamford, Connecticut

Stand-Up Guy

I was still a newlywed when I accidentally stood my mother-in-law up for lunch. The next time I went to visit her she gave me a really hard time. I mentioned the incident to my husband Phil when I came home, swearing to him I absolutely, positively just forgot. I assured him that it wasn't because I didn't want to have lunch with his mother; I couldn't believe it had just slipped my mind. "Don't worry about it," he assured me. A little later he announced he was stepping out to get the paper.

The next time I saw my mother-in-law, she said, "Boy, I can't say anything bad about you."

I found out Phil had gone straight to his mother and took *my* side. To this day no one will tell me what he said, but whatever it was made all the difference.

- Brandy, Bangor, Maine

LOSER

Roll Over Boy

I dumped Andrew after I met his super-WASPy mother. She disliked that I was Italian. That I was also half Irish and Catholic only made things worse.

One night we were gathered at his parents' place for a family dinner. Some of her grandchildren were there, and because it was close to Halloween, they were in costumes. One kid came up to me and asked, "Miss Colleen"—she made all of the children call me Miss Colleen—"What are you going to be for Halloween?"

Not giving it much thought, I quickly said, "I'm going to be a bunny."

And then I heard his mother say, "Amateur or professional?"

I laughed it off because I didn't know what else to do. But Andrew sat there like a stone. That's when I ended things. I couldn't respect a man who'd let his mother insult me.

- Colleen, Bridgeport, Connecticut

KEEPER

You're Always Beautiful, Darlin'

For the longest time after my daughter was born she was absolutely bald. I mean like a cue ball. I joked around that if she was still hairless by her first birthday I would cut my hair off in sympathy. Meanwhile I was approaching 40 and felt like I could use a change. Sure enough, Franny was about to turn 1 and was still bald. So while my husband, Will, was away on business, I just went and cut all my hair off. Now Will had *only* known me with long hair. In fact he often commented on how beautiful he thought it was.

The night I knew he was coming home, I darkened the house (probably not just to be romantic but so he wouldn't see me as clearly), lit candles, and put on velvet leggings and a lace top. When I answered the door I could see his eyes go wide—he almost looked like he thought he was at the wrong house. He sort of gulped and sputtered, "Gee, you look great." (I realized later that he hadn't said a word about my *hair* looking great.)

Two years later when my hair had mostly grown back, and I made some comment about how I liked it better longer, he finally admitted to me, "Honey, I *hated* your short hair, but I love you."

- Tracy, Los Angeles, California

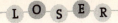

Clothes Make the Woman

I was briefly—let me emphasize *briefly*—dating a guy who either liked the trailer trash look or something really hippie. I'm a Banana Republic–type myself.

One day he suggested I change my look.

"I don't have a problem with my look," I replied. "You do!"

It took about two more weeks to say the final farewell, but that was the defining moment when I realized that he had no respect for who I am—and worse, wanted me dressed like a tramp.

- Micky, Atlanta, Georgia

KEEPER

Not Such a Macho, Macho Man

Jack seemed a little macho to me when we started dating. But I saw a different side to him when his sister and brother-in-law brought their newborn son from Toronto to meet the family. We were having lunch at his parents' apartment. Not long after we finished, Jack left me at the table to go into the bathroom with his sister and new nephew. I got up after a while, and I found him in the bathroom cooing to his nephew while giving him a bath. It was the most adorable thing to watch this 25 year old talking baby talk and cuddling a baby. I thought, *Oh my! This guy is great daddy material.*

- Lynn, Newport, Rhode Island

LOSER

A Total Mamma's Boy

I met Joe, an engineer, through a personals ad. Low key and basically decent, he was 41, never married, and had apparently had only one long-term relationship. When I commented on his lifetime of singleness, he remarked that he didn't think there was anything to be concerned with, though if he wasn't married by the time he was 50, he might start to think about why that was. A friend pointed out that he was giving himself *nine* more years.

I ignored the signals. We'd been seeing each other every weekend when I asked if we were going to get together on Valentine's Day. He declined, saying, "I always spend Valentine's Day with my mother." That's when I dumped him.

- Carin, St. Paul, Minnesota

KEEPER

He's the Cat's Meow

On Memorial Day we had to put one of our two precious cats to sleep. My husband, Dan, and I had purchased two Maine Coone kittens, littermates, when they were only 12 weeks old. We named them Rusty and Bogie, and they were truly part of the family. Even though Bogie was 11, we were both devastated when he died. Dan was surprised at how hard it hit him. The following Wednesday I had to make a big presentation in the afternoon at the advertising agency where I work. I was nervous and distracted. Dan rescheduled his patients (he's a dermatologist) and went to a wonderful store in our neighborhood called the Clay Pot. He bought me a beautiful necklace and earrings to match the outfit I had on. (I hadn't even bothered to put on jewelry.) He showed up at my office ten minutes before my presentation and gave me the gift, saying, "I know you feel rotten about Bogie. Now go break a leg."

- Felica, Park Slope, New York

LOSER

Dog-Gone It!

I'd been dating a psychologist for several months and cared deeply for him. I thought we communicated fairly well. After all, he was a shrink and dealt with people with all sorts of problems every day. But each time we started to talk about our future together, he would say, "I really need to reflect on this." He claimed it would be easier to express his feelings in a letter.

In my sense of things, this letter was going to be a marriage proposal or something about taking the next step in our relationship.

I waited and waited for the letter. And at last, he slipped me this fat little envelope after we'd been out on a date. I thought, *Okay, this is what I've been waiting for*. I drove home and opened the letter—it truly was reams.

Shocked doesn't begin to describe my feelings. The whole letter was about . . . his dog. It seems that his golden retriever had gotten lost at his house in the mountains, and after weeks the dog still hadn't been found. For five pages my psychologist boyfriend went on about how this had mired him in a deep depression, and he couldn't move forward. There wasn't a single word in the letter about our relationship. Obviously this was the end of the road for me. It still boggles me that we were on such different wavelengths.

- Sarah, Fort Collins, Colorado

KEEPER

Love Me, Love My (Old) Dog

Shortly after John moved in we came home from work to find that my very old chocolate Labrador retriever was having trouble breathing. We rushed him over to the vet. After they x-rayed Campbell, the doctor came to talk to us. Very gently, he explained that Labradors could be expected to live twelve to fourteen years, and Campbell was already 15.

The vet said, "It would be ethical, logical to put him to sleep." He told us we had a choice: put the dog to sleep or take him to the Animal Medical Center in Manhattan, where we should be prepared to spend thousands of dollars for an operation that *might* save the dog. We'd been saving for a vacation. I knew if Campbell had an operation, we wouldn't be able to afford to go. Without missing a beat, John asked, "How late is the Animal Medical Center open?"

That night it cost us $4,800 to save Campbell!

P.S. When we were robbed a few weeks later, Campbell managed to jump into the bathtub to hide!

- Hope, Providence, Rhode Island

Man's Best Friend

I called home one day to talk to my boyfriend and got the answering machine. Since I rarely called home I'd never heard the message before. It said, "You've reached Chris, Bailey, and Annette."

Bailey is the dog.

When I got home, I asked Chris why the dog's name was ahead of mine on the message. And he actually said, "Because he's more important."

• Annette, Colorado Springs, Colorado

KEEPER

Food for Thought

We were budding "foodies" celebrating our third wedding anniversary in Paris. For our special dinner we went to an exclusive restaurant (La Photogalerie) on Ile St. Louis. My husband, Paul, who writes about beer, was jet-lagged and unsure of his French. He kept his order simple: boeufsteak bleu, salade vert, pommes frites, and a carafe of vin ordinare. I was determined to practice my French and order something special. I knew *veau* was veal and surmised that *rognon* was something round like a medallion. Medallion of veal. Sounded good. When dinner was served, there in the center of my plate was a perfectly steamed artichoke set in mustard sauce amid a very large number of very small lamb kidneys. (Yuck!) Seeing the look on my face, Paul silently offered his dinner and took mine.

He says he loved my meal. But I loved *him* for the gesture.

- Ginny, Newport, Rhode Island

LOSER

Feeding Frenzy

Zach was the messiest eater in the world. Every time we'd go out there'd be mayonnaise on his chin, mustard on his tie, ketchup on his cheek. It got to the point where I couldn't go out to eat with him. I just lost my appetite.

- Jackie, Chicago, Illinois

KEEPER

The Way to *My* Heart . . .

My future husband did not look like the man of my dreams, but when he asked me out, I figured *what the hell?* He asked me out on our first date by handing me his card. It invited me to breakfast at his apartment. He listed the menu as "bacon, scrambled eggs, toast, and me." I thought that was endearing.

As we dated, he continued to woo me with food. He knew I loved Häagen-Dazs ice cream. We thought it was kind of elite because it was manufactured in Europe. (Remember, it had the little map of Oslo, Stockholm, and Copenhagen on it.) He spent two weeks tracking down where it came from—until he discovered it was actually made in the Bronx! At the time it was only sold in one store in Manhattan, but he found a distributor and courted me with pints of Häagen-Dazs rum raisin ice cream.

(By the way, I still have the card!)

- Peggy, Riverdale, New York

LOSER

Who Does Chicken Right?

I'd been dating a guy for about two years who was eighteen years older than me. He was athletic, but also a little pudgy—maybe twenty-five pounds overweight. I'd recently gotten interested in elite physical fitness—I'm a body builder—and as a result his overeating and poor table manners were starting to bug me. One day as we were driving, he said, "Oh! We just passed my favorite chicken place. We've got to go back and get some of that chicken."

I wasn't hungry. It was 11 AM. We'd just had breakfast. But he was determined to get the chicken. So we were eating in the car, and he was licking his chops. I thought, *How many thousands of meals will I eat with my mate over the course of a lifetime?* I figured if I couldn't make it through this one, I wasn't going to make it with this guy long term. Shortly after the Chicken Episode I ended things.

- Bronna, Washington, DC

KEEPER

My Very Own Cookie Monster

We were dating for about a month when I knew I wanted to take Shelly home to meet my mother. He invited me to his apartment to help him make chocolate chip cookies for the nurses and patients at the hospital where he was an ophthalmologist. There was no special occasion; he just thought it would be a nice idea to hand cookies out after the eye examinations. I especially liked it when he told me the next evening that he offered a 5-year-old child *four* cookies because four different doctors looked at her eyes.

We got married three years ago. He doesn't bake anymore, but he does use his surgical skills to chop and dice . . . and he even cleans up!

- Bonnie, New York, New York

LOSER

The Day the Cookie Crumbled

My fiancé Chris and I both worked at one of the resorts on the Las Vegas strip. One day he caught me coming out of the employee cafeteria as he was going in. I was with a new employee, showing her around the property. I was holding a cookie I'd grabbed on the way out. I introduced Chris to the girl, and in the same breath that he said, "Nice to meet you," he turned to me and said, "You shouldn't be eating that cookie." Then he walked away. The new girl just looked at me like, *I can't believe he just said that*. I was shocked, too. Chris had never said anything to me about my weight before. To me that's a cardinal sin. You do not ever tell your fiancée—or even imply—that she's fat.

Later that night he tried to downplay it. But things were never the same after that. Those kinds of comments can really wound.

- Angela, Las Vegas, Nevada

KEEPER

When My Dad Needed Him, He Was There

My husband's relationship with my mother and father was not what I would ever call warm and fuzzy. Basically, my father had always thought I could have done better, and though he never said it outright, Phil knew how he felt. Over the years my parents were crazy about our kids but cool to Phil.

After he lost his cleaning business in the Depression (right about the time yours truly was born), my father worked for his brother manufacturing negligees for the next thirty years. About ten years before he retired they set up a partnership on one aspect of the business, so my father had some equity. The time came for my father to retire, and there were issues when my dad tried to get his share out of the business. My father didn't have a clue about how to go about negotiating with his brother. Someone needed to step in and help him make the best deal possible.

Phil, a savvy small-business owner himself, volunteered. The idea was to keep it "all in the family." Phil took a very direct role and sat in with my dad and my uncle at every meeting. In short, he made sure my father got what he deserved. It was a very modest amount of money, but it was the only nest egg my parents had after all those years. (I never knew exactly what happened at those meetings, but my father definitely had a new respect for my husband.)

Given that my parents and my husband had never been close or even talked much about business, Phil did not have to put himself out. But he did. Phil brought all of his intelligence and people skills to bear. He got my father all that was coming to him, and did so in a firm but gentlemanly manner that created dignity and respect in a situation that could easily have been ugly. I was very proud of him.

- Sarah, Newport, Rhode Island

LOSER

Like Mother, Like Girlfriend

I was dating a guy with a great mom. She was very accomplished—she had three degrees, she flew planes. But whenever he talked about her, it was always surprisingly negative. That was a telltale sign. My grandmother and mother had always told me, "Watch how your boyfriend treats his mother because that's how he'll end up treating you." Sure enough, during our relationship, he treated me badly, cheating on me with another woman. My mother *and* grandmother were right.

- Danielle, Evanston, Illinois

KEEPER

Every Night Is a Slumber Party

I had just started a new job and was scheduled to have a business lunch with an attorney I had never met. Matt and I hit it off immediately. We had dozens of things to talk and laugh about. It was really refreshing. For the first time in my life, I just enjoyed being with someone. My friendship with Matt—and that's all it was for a long time—made me realize that even though I was engaged, I deserved better.

After I called off my engagement, Matt and I got closer. It hit me during a racquetball game that I wanted to marry him. I could actually describe why I wanted to be with this person for the rest of my life. I felt so comfortable with him, and we were laughing so hard. It didn't matter at all who won, just that we were together. It came to me at that moment.

We have been married for ten years, and I feel like we are having a slumber party every night. He is still my best friend, which is how we started off.

- Angela, Upper Saddle River, New Jersey

LOSER

Motor Mouth

At one Christmas party my husband got, shall we say, inebriated, and started running off at the mouth about bedroom things— mainly, how I did not choose to "do it" as often as he'd like. He was going on and on, making fun of me. To me, sex is part of love, and if you've grown apart, you just don't do it.

At the end of the evening, we were driving home with another couple, and my husband said to the other guy, "So what did you think of the hostess?" She was a skinny blonde whom I didn't know.

"Okay, I guess," he said.

"Well, let me tell you," my husband declared, "she was one good lay. She was my girlfriend for many years, and she was better than this one."

I was furious. We'd already been having problems, but this was the breaking point. The next morning I called my mother-in-law, asked her to watch the kids, and called a lawyer. I told my husband, "You're outta here."

- Linda, Manahawkin, New Jersey

KEEPER

Your Husband Thinks You Deserve the Best

I'm not an extravagant person—not at all. But when I was younger I was completely taken with my friend's mom's beautiful Mercedes-Benz 450 SLX. When I first started dating my husband, I told him, "When I grow up, I'm going to buy myself a Mercedes."

I forgot that conversation. But three years ago I needed a car. I didn't want to spend a lot because our son had just gone off to college and we were paying tuition. I had planned to just replace my old, leased car, but they wanted to increase the interest payments.

So one day Richard called me at work to go car shopping. We stopped at a Volvo dealer and then he said, "Just for the fun of it, let's go to a Mercedes-Benz dealer." It was like fantasyland for me. I "picked out" the car of my dreams and "pretended" by going back and forth over the options. I could see the dealer was getting kind of antsy. I said, "You know it's really too much money. It doesn't fit my lifestyle."

Finally the dealer had enough. He turned to my husband and said, "Why don't you tell your wife what you told me when you came in here two weeks ago?"

I was stunned and said, "What are you talking about?"

He answered, "Mrs. E, your husband told me, 'My wife is an amazing lady. She gives everything to everyone else. She will never buy this car for herself, but we can afford it. I want to give her what she has always wanted—because she deserves the best.'"

It turned out my husband had already paid for the car. All I had to do was pick out the color.

You better believe I drive that silver Mercedes all over town.

- Leigh, Riverdale, New York

LOSER

Speak Up or Forever Hold Your Peace

My husband and I had just gotten married and were starting a new media company in our living room. About the same time a friend of mine invited me to join her on a six-day trip to Panama City, Florida. I was dying to go. I'm fascinated with dolphins, and the place she mentioned was known to have a lot of dolphins off the shoreline. I'd gone swimming with some captive dolphins in Australia as part of an undercover documentary; now I wanted to swim with them in the wild.

Because of a barter arrangement, the trip was only going to cost me $500. However, we had next to no money and were just beginning to get into what's Mine and Yours is now Ours. I wasn't asking his permission to go, but he seemed fine with the trip. The way I was brought up, if you didn't say anything, you were going along with it. But I learned much later that for him, silence was not affirmation.

The trip was a blast. I laughed nonstop, ate amazing food, and swam with the dolphins. I came back tan and rested. But when I got home, my husband had this stick up his ass sideways. Only he wasn't saying that.

"What's up?" I asked.

"Nothing," he said, then blurted, "but I just want to tell you that I bought a software program for producing albums on a Mac for $5,000, and we're going to go into business with this."

Then he came out with this psycho business plan that he'd never discussed with me even though we were supposed to be partners. It took about a week for me to realize that this was the revenge for my going away and having an incredible time without him. That was the moment when I saw the guy's true colors. He not only got pissed off, he got pissed off a zero more.

Cady, New York, New York

KEEPER

Isn't It Romantic?

The night of April 26, 2002, reinforced without a doubt all my beliefs that my boyfriend Jared is a Keeper. We had planned a long weekend in San Diego so that we could see one of his clients tape a television show. As we approached San Diego, he told me, less than pleased, that we had to stop at his client's hotel to pick up more copies of her books so that she could distribute them at the taping.

We pulled up to this gorgeous resort and spa overlooking the ocean. He parked the car and told me to wait while he grabbed the books. He returned from the hotel looking angry and proceeded to tell me that we had missed the taping because his client didn't inform him about a change in the schedule. As I tried to calm him down, he asked if I would mind spending some time with his client and her husband in their room before heading to our hotel for dinner. I agreed and then did my best to keep up with him, because when he is annoyed, he walks miles ahead of me.

We approached his client's room, and Jared knocked on the door, but there was no answer. He proceeded to knock again. We waited patiently. Then he pulled out a room key from his pocket, explaining that his client left him the key in case she was out on the balcony and didn't hear him.

As we entered, my eyes were drawn to the red rose petals that so sweetly covered the floor. Then I took in the whole room: there were two beautiful vases of flowers in one corner and in another corner was chilled champagne accompanied by two glasses. Candles illuminated the room from all sides and there were chocolate-covered strawberries on the dresser to my left. I was absolutely shocked and amazed. Finally Jared said, "There was no taping or client this weekend." Then he proceeded to get down on one knee and proposed!

- Diana, Los Angeles, California

LOSER

Wedding Bell Blues

At first my husband seemed great. Alain was French, and shortly after we met, he proposed a romantic trip to Paris. When I was evicted from my apartment, he just assumed that I'd move in with him—we hadn't even been dating that long. For a while it was all, *I'm in love, I'm in love.*

And then we got married.

Our wedding day was horrible. We were married at City Hall, then had a luncheon and drove to a bed and breakfast. Over dinner, all Alain kept talking about was how hot it was, how tired he was, and how he was really looking forward to going to sleep. I was sure I was going to start crying. This was our wedding day! If nothing else, I thought, I'll just get drunk. But I had to bully Alain to get the waiter to bring champagne to our room. It was all downhill from there.

- Marion, New York, New York

KEEPER

His Home, Sweet Home

Scott had purchased the house of his dreams just before we met. He worked many years to get the down payment. We had been dating about three months when I helped him paint the house, so I knew how much it meant to him. Now he was planning a big housewarming party including students and teachers from the university where he worked. The week before the party he asked, "What would you say if I asked you to marry me at the party?" I answered, "I would probably say yes, but you'll have to ask me to find out."

The night of the party I realized he was avoiding me. Wherever I was, he wasn't. I could tell he was just plain scared. I finally walked over to him and said, "Hi. Remember me?"

He turned pale. "I just can't do it—you know, ask you to marry me," he said.

I said, "It's okay. It wasn't my idea."

Then he just grabbed me, kissed me, and asked me to marry him. Then he made an announcement to everyone. He told the crowd how much he loved me and that we were going to be married. What was so sweet was that he thought about it, and even though he *was* scared, he was willing to share his feelings about it. (For one thing he was scared because of our state's community property laws! If we ever split up I would be entitled to half of his dreamhouse.) I loved that he wasn't embarrassed to come right out with it. It's been nineteen years, and we still live in that house.

- Toni, Galveston, Texas

LOSER

Who's Been Sleeping in My Bed?

Things had been kind of up and down with my boyfriend James. I hadn't heard from him in about two weeks. But at the time I didn't think anything about it; I just figured he was giving me some space because I was studying hard for my master's degree exam.

The day after the exam—I passed—I dropped by his apartment. When he opened the door, he looked flustered. Clearly he hadn't expected to see me. And when I looked past him into his apartment, it looked different—there was a new bed, a fish tank, and a brand new stereo.

What was with all the new furniture? Apparently in the two weeks I had been studying for my exam, he'd not only met someone else, but she'd moved in with him. In fact, he was expecting her when I knocked on the door.

"Why didn't you say anything?" I demanded.

"You were taking your exam," he said. "I didn't want to bother you."

- Anika, Philadelphia, Pennsylvania

KEEPER

The Sky's the Limit

A couple of years ago I was coming home from a hiking trip in Utah. I was supposed to meet up with my husband, Mac, in Toronto where he was planning to wind up on a business trip. The plan was for me to fly into Chicago and change planes for Toronto. Unfortunately, there was a terrible rainstorm and flooding in the Chicago area. The airport closed down; there were no flights out and no hotel rooms. When I finally reached my husband I said, "They are saying that the earliest we'll get out is Tuesday." This was Saturday night.

A few planes did manage to take off the next morning. Each time a plane's departure would be announced, a bunch of us would dash over to see if we could get a seat. No luck. Finally it was announced that a flight was leaving for Toronto. When we got to the gate, they made an announcement that only people with tickets for *that flight* could get on. Again people were getting in line anyway. As each person got to the gate, they would be turned away. I handed my original ticket to the guy and waited to be turned away, but he said, "Okay, there you go." There were no reserved seats on this flight, so I just sat where I could. I was nervously waiting for someone to come and drag me off, since I knew I didn't have a ticket for that particular flight.

When I got to Toronto, my husband was right there waiting for me at the gate. What I couldn't figure out was how he knew which flight I was on. Apparently the previous night he had connected with a ticket agent from United Airlines and he actually had been tracking me. Every time a plane took off from the Chicago airport, this woman would check to see if I was on it. She finally booked me on the flight to Toronto, then she called to tell Mac exactly when I was coming in. Mac took me to the hotel, ordered me breakfast, then tucked me in, kissed me, and went off to conduct business in Toronto.

- Lisa, Seattle, Washington

LOSER

I Do, I Don't

I decided that my husband was a huge Loser the day of our wedding.

I'd put a lot of time and thought into our big day. I'd had my hair and makeup professionally done. I'd spent $1,500 on a dress. We were to take our pictures in a beautiful park before the wedding so that after the ceremony we could go right to the party and have some fun. My best friend and I were at the hotel where we had gotten ready, and the van that was to take us to the park was late. When we finally got to the park, everyone else in the bridal party was there. The first thing my husband-to-be, Don, said to me was, "Why the fuck are you late?" Not, "You look beautiful." Not, "I love you." Not, "What a wonderful day this is going to be." No. He says, "Why the fuck are you late?"

It's fair to say that I cried the whole way down the aisle. Of course everyone thought I was crying because I was so happy. But I knew it was all wrong.

- Kira, Yorba Linda, California

KEEPER

The Final Goodbye

When my sister passed away in 1978 I said good-bye to her at the funeral, sat shiva, went to the unveiling, and then never, ever returned to the cemetery to visit her grave. Over the years I would get very depressed and cry over the Fourth of July weekend, because that was the last weekend I spent with her before she died. When I met Sam, I told him all about my sister and how, although I had "officially" said good-bye at the cemetery, there was still some unfinished business in my heart. One of the first things he suggested after our first Fourth of July together was that we take a trip to the cemetery where Shelly was buried. At the cemetery I had a really good cry, introduced Sam to Shelly, and then finally said a proper good-bye to her.

I knew he was a Keeper on our first date, but his knowledge of my need to say farewell and close an open wound really sealed it for me.

- Laney, Omaha, Nebraska

LOSER

Terms of Endearment

My fiancé and I met about six weeks after my sister had had a bone marrow transplant. She had leukemia and, after the transplant, was in the hospital for three months. Brad would pick me up at the hospital, take me to dinner, and bring me back. He met my sister—I wanted her to know the person I was going to spend the rest of my life with. She loved him.

When Michelle died in December 1999, Brad and I had been together for more than a year. He came with me to the hospital and was with me when she took her last breath.

Even though I no longer had to care for Michelle, after she died there was still a lot to do. I helped her husband, Joe, clean out the closets and helped take care of her kids. I was at Joe's every weekend, and I talked with him every day. It was a way of maintaining the connection with my sister.

The problem was Brad assumed that after Michelle's death we'd just magically move on with our lives together. But I was having a lot of trouble getting over Michelle's death. Every day I'd come home depressed with red, swollen eyes. But I don't remember him once asking me how things were going or whether I was thinking about Michelle. He couldn't talk about it with me; he just wanted to sweep it under the rug. He kept saying, "It's time to get over this."

Finally I took some vacation time and went to California to visit my mom. While I was out there, I decided to break off the relationship. I called Brad and said, "Listen, when I get home, I'm going to move out. This is a major thing, and I'm not going to get over it."

I will say this: Brad was great about the breakup. He packed up all of my things and moved me into my new apartment. I didn't have to lift a finger. I always say he's a really nice guy. He's just not *my* nice guy.

- Connie, Washington, DC

He Could Be Silly

Marshall and I had just started living together. He's a playwright and on the "serious" side. One day we went to visit my aunt and her 2-year-old granddaughter. We were strolling around the town green when we came upon a thrift shop with a big stuffed bear in the window. Marshall slipped into the store, got into the window, and made the bear wave to the toddler. She was absolutely delighted. My aunt turned to me and said, "What a dear, sweet man!"

- Marcy, Stamford, Connecticut

LOSER

Muppet Love Affair

Mike and I had been dating long distance for a while when we decided to go to Mexico together. Oddly, when Mike met me at the airport, he had a shark puppet with him. Odder still, he started talking to me *through* the shark puppet. It was something he learned in therapy with his ex-wife. He used the puppet to broach difficult or sensitive subjects. First, it was, "I missed you" and "I love you." But as we got into the trip, he used the puppet to talk about why he couldn't sustain his erection.

The whole thing was more than weird. At one point during an argument I slammed some books on a table. The puppet was underneath the books. Mike went ballistic, claiming I had hurt the puppet. I didn't hurt the puppet. It was furry and floppy. But clearly for him the puppet had a personality.

I hope the two of them are very happy together.

- Hildy, Washington, DC

KEEPER

XXXOOO Marks the Spot

Sam was in the Caribbean on his first vacation in years, and he wasn't around for Valentine's Day. But he had arranged to have flowers sent to me before he left. When I got them, I couldn't imagine who had sent them because I wasn't seeing anyone. When I opened the card, I melted. It said, "Dear Katy, I may be getting a tan, but you are getting flowers. XXXOOO Love, Sam."

We'd been co-workers and then let's-have-lunch-together friends for about a year. I had always wanted more, but he had played it so cool that I thought he wasn't interested in being anything but friends. It wasn't until the flowers arrived that I was sure the attraction was reciprocated. I've kept that card—and him.

- Katy, Knoxville, Tennessee

The Penis Monologues

A guy responded to my profile on Match.com by sending me his penis measurements. I shot back another email, asking if he was expecting my vagina measurements.

He wrote back, "No, they're all the same."

- Corday, New York, New York

KEEPER

Leader of the Pack

I was working as a parole officer in Pensacola, Florida. One night my friend Molly called me at 11:30 PM to cajole me into going out. "We'll never meet guys at home," she said. We decided to head over to a local club where you could sometimes meet cool officers who wandered in from the Air Force base. After about an hour, Rob, a photographer for a famous boxer who had a match that weekend, walked in with a friend.

He came over and we started to dance and talk. He was a very assertive take-charge guy, kind of in my face, but in a nice way. As he talked excitedly he swept my rum and tonic right into my lap. I should have been pissed off, but I wasn't. He went and got a waitress to come over with a towel—he didn't want a man mopping up my lap! Since the bar was located in a hotel, he even managed to get an iron from housekeeping and someone ironed my skirt while I was in the ladies room.

For the next few weeks he plied me with dinners and flowers and stayed in touch when he had to go home to California where the boxer also lived. But I knew from the first night that he was a gentleman. It was evident he was going to take care of me. And after twenty-three years he still does.

- Milly, Palo Alto, California

LOSER

Fight Club

Years ago when I was still in college, my boyfriend Leo and I were in bed, arguing. We'd gone to see a movie about apartheid in South Africa earlier in the evening and ended up discussing racism in America. My take was that America's race problem was in some ways more insidious because it was more covert, that despite the lip service paid to "equality," people of color often remained disadvantaged.

Leo, who was a lot older than me, long out of school and working as an editor at one of the local newspapers, *vehemently* disagreed.

I love a lively debate, particularly one about key issues. But this was getting out of control. Leo was becoming more agitated as the conversation progressed. Suddenly, after one comment I made that I guess really pissed him off, his arm swung back, his palm open, hanging menacingly in the air. He was so angry, he was shaking. His face had gone deep red. In a flash I realized that it was taking everything he had not to smack me hard.

In that moment, it was all over. If we couldn't discuss a movie without him becoming violent, what would happen later on when we disagreed about real things? The next day I packed up all of the stuff he'd left at my place, returned it to him, and told him we were through.

- Nancy, Cleveland, Ohio

KEEPER

Maid to Order

Our family tradition at Thanksgiving is to create our Christmas lists right after dinner. For several years, my list had facetiously included "a maid"—as a wife and full-time working mother of two small children, I found it very difficult to be Superwoman. Life being what it is, we could not afford the luxury of a housekeeper at that time in our lives. One day after coming home from a hectic day of work, I walked into my house and found my husband, pants rolled up to his knees, a towel around his waist like an apron, standing there with a feather duster. He said to me, "I hope you like your new maid!" The best thing was that supper was made, the wash was done, and the floors were vacuumed. Since that time we have divided up the chores equally within the family.

- Ellen, Flint, Michigan

LOSER

Not Maid for Each Other

I was having problems with my landlord, so my boyfriend asked me to move in with him. That was very sweet. His apartment, however, was disgusting. He never cleaned the kitchen. There was dirt everywhere. I couldn't live like that. But I liked this guy a lot and appreciated his generosity, so I started cleaning up a bit. He seemed really grateful. But after a few weeks, he said, "You're not cleaning as much as you used to. Since you're staying here for nothing, I think you should be cleaning more."

I couldn't believe he said that. It was one thing to clean up to be nice, but it was another to be *expected* to do it, like I was the maid. I was furious. I left immediately and went to stay with friends.

- Nancy, Queens, New York

KEEPER

Calling Mr. Mom

Just after the birth of our son, my husband, Tim, was unexpectedly laid off from his job as a truck driver.

"Don't look for a job," I told him. "I'll work full time."

Now he helps with homework and takes Greg to school. I will never forget Parents' Night at school in first grade. When I walked in, the teacher was a little surprised. After I introduced myself, she said, "Gee, I never knew Greg had a *mother*."

My husband is always there for us, and always will be.

- Patricia, Litchfield, Connecticut

LOSER

Ozzie Seeks Harriet

I thought John was going to be The Guy. We'd been dating for about a year, and he embodied everything I was looking for. He was from a fabulously wealthy family, was handsome and brilliant, had a great sense of humor, and was very intellectual, which is most important to me.

Then in one afternoon I realized that I couldn't possibly spend my life with him.

We'd finished playing tennis and were lying around talking about what we were going to do for dinner. Usually we went out. But as we were lying there, and I was thinking about where I'd like to go, he said, "I'd like you to get used to cooking dinner for me on a regular basis and having things ready for me. I'm really looking for someone who's going to take care of me."

He said it in a light way, but I knew at that moment that what he wanted was a "wife" in the classic sense of the word—not a partner or a good friend. At the time I thought it was funny, but as he was telling me this, I knew it would never work. At least he was honest, and he picked his moment to lay out his terms. But that was it for me.

- Pam, Westport, Connecticut

KEEPER

Daddy's Here

When I finally got pregnant after years of trying and fertility treatments, it was like a miracle. I was carrying twins. Philip was glued to the Internet looking for information about pregnancy and baby development. He read somewhere that babies' brains begin to develop in utero and that you should talk to them. So he would talk to my stomach. He had a line he would sing all the time: "Daddy's here, and dad-dy loves you. Yes. Yes. Yes."

When it came time to deliver, I had a C-section. First they took out Janie. Two minutes later came Maddy. Each twin had her own pediatrician and her own team. There were two bassinets, and the doctors were poking and prodding each newborn. It turned out that Maddy needed a little more monitoring. As each team was trying hard to console a crying twin, Philip left my side and stood right between the two bassinets. Then he started to sing, "Daddy's here, and dad-dy loves you. Yes. Yes. Yes."

They both stopped crying instantly.

- Fran, Baton Rouge, Louisiana

LOSER

Three's a Crowd

I'd been dating this seemingly great guy I'd met in a nightclub for about six months when he started talking about getting engaged. Everything was perfect, except that I'd never been to his house. He was always at my place. Ron's excuse was that I lived close to where he worked, so it was just easier to come to my house. But I thought it was strange after six months and a promise of engagement that I still didn't know where he lived.

About that time I ran into a mutual friend who told me that Ron already had a live-in girlfriend. Impossible, I said. He's at my house every night till 3 AM. There's just no way.

But certain things weren't adding up, so I decided to check it out. I found out where he lived and went to his house, and what do you know ... a woman was living there with his *two kids* from a previous marriage. Funny, he'd never mentioned them either.

I was hysterical. His story was that their relationship was over, that she was just living there because she didn't have another place to live. I gave him one month to have her out of there. But at the end of the month, she was still there. This time I went and talked with her. She told me that as far as she knew there was nothing wrong with their relationship, that they've been together for eight years. I pointed out that for the last six months he'd been at my house. Where did she think he was? Apparently his excuse for not being home was that he traveled a lot.

"I don't see what the problem is," Ron said, trying to justify the whole situation when I confronted him. "I spend all of my time with you anyway." Then the kicker, "Plus, we'll already have somebody to look after the kids."

On the spot, I told him to take a hike.

- Sheryl, Capetown, South Africa

KEEPER

There's Still an "Us"

Around the time of our wedding anniversary my husband's 27-year-old son from his first marriage died in a car accident when he fell asleep at the wheel. Glen went to Detroit for the funeral. We discussed it and decided for several reasons—including the financial realities—that I would stay home. We needed the money from my job—I was a salesperson and I only got paid if I worked. Glen was also planning to take time off after the funeral and spend it with his other son. The day of our anniversary I walked into work, and there were a dozen roses waiting for me with the simple note, "Happy Anniversary. I love you. Glen." I hadn't expected anything. He lost his son, and yet he remembered us.

- Candy, Las Vegas, Nevada

LOSER

Father Doesn't Know Best

About five months after my husband, Alan, and I had our baby, I offered to take Lisa, his daughter from his first marriage, out to shop for a new TV for her room.

Lisa, then 8, seemed nervous, but when she saw that the baby was asleep, she reluctantly agreed to go. Not twenty minutes into our shopping trip, she started fidgeting and insisted we go home. I couldn't figure out what was wrong since I knew she really wanted a TV. Finally she burst into tears and said she was afraid that when the baby woke up, her dad would pretend he didn't hear him.

I was stunned. How did she know this? When she was a toddler, she told me, she'd watched her dad pretend to be asleep many times while she stood in her crib and begged for him to pick her up. When her mom came home, he'd say he hadn't heard her crying.

Sure enough, the baby was fussing in his crib when Lisa and I got home. When I asked Alan why he hadn't gone in to check on the baby, he said that he must have fallen asleep and didn't hear him.

Alan never improved, not one bit. I knew for certain that day that I could never depend on him as a father.

- Rachel, St. Louis, Missouri

KEEPER

Boy, Oh Boy, Oh Boy

After nine years of marriage and two kids, my husband and I hurried to the hospital for the birth of our third child. My husband was recovering from a fairly recent bout of pneumonia that had hit him hard, and wasn't feeling well. We made it to the hospital with just twenty minutes to spare. The delivery was fairly quick, and we had another boy. After the nurses and doctors left us alone for a while, and I was holding my third son, my husband, who is a man of very few words, looked at the baby and then at me and said, "I love you. You make beautiful babies."

That's something I will never forget.

- Elaine, Austin, Texas

Boys to Men

I'd known my first husband, Ryan, since we were 13. We were high school sweethearts. I would have gone through hot coals, broken glass, anything for him. But when he turned 30, he started cheating. We went to counseling, separated once, and then reconciled and were together for three more years. Then I found out he was cheating again. I would have done anything to get him back . . . until our son started having problems. I took my son to see a therapist, and the therapist wanted both my husband and I to participate. Ryan refused.

"I'm not asking you to do this for me. I'm asking you to do this for our son," I told him.

He wanted no part of it. "Tell him to be a man," he said.

"He's an 8-year-old boy!" I said hotly. "He doesn't have to be a man. He's a *little boy*."

From that moment on, there was nothing my husband could have said or done to get me back. He took our problems out on our child. That was it.

- Louise, Long Beach Island, New Jersey

KEEPER

I Was the Envy of Every Other Woman

It was a Saturday, and I was getting my hair done in a salon around the corner from my apartment. Suddenly it began to pour. A collective groan went up throughout the salon. I considered calling my husband, Daniel, to see if he would bring the car around, but I was embarrassed to bother him. I'd just decided to wait out the rain, when suddenly there he was in the doorway with an umbrella.

"I didn't want you to get your hair wet," he mumbled.

It was one of the few times in my life that I knew I was the envy of a roomful of women. As I hugged him, he said, "Remember this when I forget to take the garbage out."

To myself I thought, "I'll take a man with an umbrella any day."

- Luci, Bozeman, Montana

LOSER

Will the Real Marcia Please Stand Up?

I was dating an older guy, a real sweet-talker. We'd been out on two dates when he took me to a party his friends were having. All night all I kept hearing was, "So, you're Marcia. It's so nice to finally meet you!"

I thought, *Wow! This guy must really like me. He's talked about me to all of his friends.*

Then somebody said to me, "Didn't you just celebrate an anniversary? You've been married, what, five years or something?"

Turns out that his *wife's* name was also Marcia. And he just carried it off like, "This is Marcia." Everyone thought *I* was his wife. Of course I had no idea he was married. But as soon as I found out, I insisted he take me home.

- Marcia, Manahawkin, New Jersey

KEEPER

Mr. Mary Poppins

My husband has an 18-year-old daughter whom he raised on his own—all on a policeman's salary. There was no child support from his ex. When we got married, he made it clear he didn't want any more kids. However, I was on the fence about the issue, and then, of course, right after we got married, I changed my mind. So when I told him I wanted a baby, we agreed that because he didn't want one, I would do 80 percent of the work.

And then Max was born, and I was absolutely exhausted. Guess what? Carl, without once complaining, did everything. He changed diapers. He got up in the middle of the night. He was there when *we* needed him.

- Faith, Westchester, New York

LOSER

No Kid-ding Around

My live-in boyfriend Geoff and I were spending the weekend with his best friends Annie and Jim. I'd always gotten along fine with them, but Annie was pregnant when we were visiting, and the moment we got there, she started in on me about how Geoff and I had to have a baby. Why is it that new moms or moms-to-be always assume that everyone should have kids? *My* friends know I don't want children. I've *never* wanted children. And it was no secret to Geoff that I didn't want to have a baby.

It had been a long drive to see them, and later on, I excused myself to take a nap. But I could hear them talking in the next room. Annie was going on and on to Geoff about how I had to have a baby and how I'm horrible if I don't want to have a baby. I was annoyed at her for pursuing the topic even after I'd explained that kids just weren't for me. But I was furious at Geoff. He just sat there and didn't say a word to defend me.

- Joanna, Portland, Oregon

KEEPER

He *Loves* His Cars, but He Loves Me More

Harry, my husband, loves his cars. He treats them like pets. He names each one and worries about the first ding. Over the years I have had my share of accidents. Never once did he yell at me. Last week I had a bad fender bender in our new black Mercedes. I called him up at work. The first question he asked was, "Are you sure *you're* okay?"

- Helene, Great Neck, New York

LOSER

Crash and Burn

I loved riding around on Rob's classic Harley. But on this particular night, I didn't realize how much he'd had to drink or I'd have never gotten on the bike.

We were about a half-mile from my house, and he was going pretty fast when I saw that the light ahead was red. I remember thinking, *It'll turn green by the time we get there*. In fact, what turned green was the left-turn arrow. The car in front of us turned, and Rob swerved, but we still slammed into it. My leg was crushed between the bike and the car. Fortunately the guy we hit was an emergency medical technician. He wasn't hurt, and he helped me until the ambulance arrived.

I spent ten days in the hospital and, in that time, I had three surgeries on my leg. When I got out, I had three more. At first the doctors didn't think they'd be able to save my leg. Later I found out that they didn't think I'd ever walk again. I was on crutches for two years, but eventually I walked.

Rob was in the same hospital. He wasn't hurt nearly as badly as I was, but he never came to see me.

Months passed, and Rob still didn't call. I needed to get some closure on the accident, so I paged him. He agreed to meet me, but when we finally got together, it was clear he didn't want to deal with the accident.

"You need to show me you feel some kind of regret," I told him.

"You know I really love you," he responded.

That certainly wasn't what I expected. I was speechless.

"*Excuse me?*" I demanded. "Your answer is you love me? Not, 'I'm sorry?' Not, 'What can I do to help, even if it's not much?' All you do is say you love me? Unbelievable."

He still had no answer.

I called him an asshole and crutched my way out the door.

Karla, Wichita, Kansas

KEEPER

He Digs Deep and Finds More

My husband, who is a conservation officer with a K-9 shepherd named Jazz, was sent to New York City to help out soon after 9/11. He did not take Jazz with him but left him in my care. At that time we had just sent our oldest daughter to college three hundred miles away from home, and our 15-year-old was at home with me. I was busy with school and soccer games. I also had my mom nearby in an assisted living facility. Plus I was working full time so, needless to say, I had a full plate trying to keep the home fires going and continue a sense of normalcy for the family.

One night, around 1 AM, my husband returned from the city after a very difficult week. I was leaving early the next day for a conference about two hours from home. When I got to the conference, I had an urgent message to call home. The assisted living facility had called; my mom had had a stroke and was being taken to the local hospital. I immediately headed home. When I arrived at the hospital, I found my husband with my mom, talking to her, stroking her arm and providing her comfort. My mom never recovered consciousness and passed away within days. I was so impressed that my husband went directly to my mom after the experience he had just been through. I know that this man will always be there for me and our children.

- Lyn, Lyme, Connecticut

LOSER

Liar, Liar

Todd seemed like a great guy, but he had a habit of telling these outrageous stories. It wasn't that I ever caught him in a lie, but there was just no way that everything he told me could be true. For instance, he'd ask me out, then not show up. Then he'd call with a wild tale like his sister had been diagnosed with breast cancer. Another time, the story was that he was divorced, his ex-wife committed suicide, and he had to go to California for her funeral. Then his mother was deathly ill, his sister was in the hospital, he got into a bar fight . . .

It just didn't make sense. There was no way a person could have this much bad luck. I decided the guy was weird and that I wasn't going to go out with him anymore.

A few months later I heard from him again. He told me that he had become a fireman and that he'd gone into a burning building, the second floor fell on him, and he'd been in the hosptial for four days. I didn't believe that at all. I didn't think that they'd send a rookie into a burning building. Strangely, it's not like he ever wanted to be a fireman, but he told me that he remembered how much *I* liked firemen, and thought it would be the ideal thing for him to do to win me back. That's when I thought he was literally crazy. I said, "Don't take this personally, but I never want to speak to you again."

Funny, he really did become a fireman. That was probably the one thing that was true.

- Jackie, Brooklyn, New York

KEEPER

My Own Private Kinkos

A dream project I had landed turned into a nightmare that was taking up all my time, forcing me to turn down other work in my communications business. After about six weeks I realized that despite a contract with the client, I would have to resign to save my sanity and my business.

I phoned the client and informed her that I would be unable to continue, but she kept insisting that we were nearly done and that she was sending me the tiny remaining sections so I could tell her exactly *when* I would finish. Taken off guard, I hung up the phone feeling like a black cloud was hanging over me. The unresolved situation had me in tears. I called my husband, who was enjoying a vacation day at a friend's house. He convinced me that I had to call the client back immediately and tell her firmly that I could no longer continue the project under any circumstance and not to send me any additional material. He helped me role-play just what I would say.

His approach worked, and by the time he came home at noon, I had successfully resigned. However, since I was breaking a contract, I realized I needed to photocopy about three hundred pages of the work I had done before returning all the material to the client. This was my only proof of having fulfilled at least part of the contract in good faith.

Jay took the stack of files from me, said he would make the copies, and returned at 5 PM with a set of duplicates, neatly arranged in sections and clipped. I was overwhelmed. "Why did you do this?" I asked him. "Because I felt so bad that you were at home crying, and I wasn't there to help. I needed to do whatever I could to help you put this behind you," he answered.

• Tanya, Park Slope, Brooklyn

LOSER

What's Your Definition of *Together*?

My (now ex-) husband and I were having an intimate dinner on Christmas Day—just the two of us at a small neighborhood restaurant. We hadn't made any elaborate holiday plans because the following day we were moving into the new home we'd recently bought. I'm still not sure how it came up, but we got to talking about past lovers. I asked if he'd slept with anyone else while we were together. "Not while we were engaged" was his Clintonian hedge.

His carefully worded response naturally made me think he'd slept with others while we were dating, perhaps living together, but not technically engaged. I pounced on the ambiguity and pried it out of him. Yes, in fact, he 'fessed up that he had spent an afternoon with a young assistant at her apartment under the guise of helping her with her resume! They'd been having lunch, she invited him back to her place, and *Whoop! There it is*.

I was crushed. He tried to brush it off, pointing out that he'd put the ring on my finger almost immediately afterward and that he'd married me, and besides it had happened well over two years ago. Well, it happened two years ago to *him*. For me his infidelity was unfolding in present time, and I was deeply hurt. What hurt even more was that he couldn't fathom that I *was* hurt. He kept saying, "What's the big deal? It happened before we were married."

All the joy of moving into our new home—my first as a homeowner—was sucked out of the moment. It took a few more years for the relationship to wholly unravel—after all, we'd just gotten married—but that's when it began to fray. Any night he didn't come home till the wee hours without calling just added to my certainty that he was fooling around again. And by a certain point, I stopped caring. Eventually I left.

Daria, Long Beach, California

KEEPER

True Lies

We were watching football together on Sunday afternoon—something we've done often during our twenty-year marriage. It was halftime and the "perfect" perky cheerleaders came out. Feeling less than perfect, I said to Matt, "I thank God you knew me back when I was in my prime and at my best."

He said, "What are you talking about? You haven't even reached your prime yet. You keep getting better with age."

He lifted my spirits just like that—even though we *both* knew he was lying through his teeth! That's a Keeper.

- Christine, Montclair, New Jersey

LOSER

Ankles Away

I had a real fixation on this guy in graduate school. We'd dated on and off, and I bumped into him on a day when I thought I looked pretty nice. I was coming out of a building and he was coming up the steps. As he saw me, he said, "You have very thick ankles. Do you come from peasant stock?" The infatuation died right there.

- Ellen, Ithaca, New York

Touched by an Angel

I have known Hugh since I was four—we practically grew up together. We went to church together. We both married, had children, and then divorced. He's godfather to my child; I'm godmother to his.

I didn't hear from him or about him for a long time—maybe ten years—but I always wondered about him. Then one Sunday I didn't go to church, and it turned out Hugh was there asking my uncle about *me*. Finally we caught up with each other.

I said, "So, do you have a new girl in your life?"

"I'm looking at her," he said, "and I'm hoping she doesn't have anyone in *her* life."

He confessed that he'd been in love with me forever. Then when we started tracking our paths, I realized that he had always been there for me. He was there at my graduation taking pictures. He was there writing me letters and encouraging me all through school. (Even my daughter said, "Ma, everyone knows Hugh is in love with you.")

He said, "You know you never had confidence in yourself. You don't believe you can do things." He kept telling me that I could do and be whatever I want. "You just need that little push."

It dawned on me: this is The One. He has always been there for me and always will be. I just didn't know it. I always had an angel looking out for me. Now I know he is the real Keeper.

- Olivia, South Orange, New Jersey

LOSER

Close Encounters

I met Tom walking down the street. We'd been walking in sync, and after laughing about it, stopped to talk. He told me he was an artist and a musician. I was intrigued. We lingered for a while, then exchanged numbers.

For our third date he invited me to his place and cooked me an elaborate dinner. To me, a sign of how much a guy likes you is how many things he's willing to chop up into a salad. The produce aisle was very well represented. He'd also lit candles all over the place. It was a very nice, romantic dinner. And he was a great cook, domestic. Another good sign.

After dinner we made love for the first time. That was great, too.

Then he dropped the bomb. "I have something to tell you."

Never good words to hear, especially after a great meal and great sex. How bad could it be? Was he married? Gay?

Any of those would have been easier to hear. He proceeded to tell me that he'd been *abducted by aliens*. From this room. From this very bed. Dozens of times over the years. His last girlfriend, he told me conspiratorily, watched it all happen—how his body would float out the window and into the spaceship. Apparently she couldn't come to his aid because she was frozen, unable to move. Afterward, he said, he couldn't remember much, but he always ended up back in bed.

I tried to pretend it was all fine. But I realized he was a total crackpot. He really believed he'd been abducted. I never saw that particular space cadet again.

- Brenda, New York, New York

KEEPER

It *Is* All Greek to Me

My elderly father just loves to listen to Greek radio stations and watch Greek television. For my dad's birthday my new boyfriend thought of the best birthday gift: a shortwave radio so dad could tune into any station he wanted. My dad has made it clear to me that I better keep this one!

- Elena, Astoria, New York

LOSER

The Fighting Irish

Bill was not a mainstream kind of guy. He rode his bike everywhere and had this sexy mountain man aura about him. I liked him because he made me laugh. But he loved to play devil's advocate, and the problem was that he didn't know when it was appropriate and when it wasn't.

We had been going out for about six months when I had my appendix removed. I was just coming out of the anesthesia when, through the fog, I saw Bill having an argument . . . with my mother . . . across my bed.

This was their first meeting. Apparently my mother had been trying to make small talk, and since they're both Irish Americans, they were talking about Ireland. My mother made some reference to the ancient kings of Ireland, and Bill challenged her. I saw her nostrils flare, which only happens when she's really angry. Her cheeks turned bright red, and she snapped back at him, essentially telling him to fuck off. I thought, *Oh, well. Scratch that one off the list.*

- Christine, Brooklyn, New York

KEEPER

He Certainly Plans to Keep Me!

Shortly before my thirty-fifth wedding anniversary I came home from work early, as I usually did on Fridays during the summer when work was just half a day. I was expecting to see Mort, my hubby, who was always off on Fridays, in the garden or just relaxing a bit. A couple of hours went by and since I was busy doing this and that, it just didn't occur to me that I hadn't heard from him. However, by late afternoon I started wondering where he'd gone since he would have left a note on the kitchen table if he had planned to be out all afternoon. I was certainly happy when I heard him whistling when he entered the house. When I told him that he had me worried, he said he didn't realize how long his errand was going to take him.

To my surprise, he'd gotten a colorful tattoo that almost encircled his entire arm. (I could look but not touch it just yet.) He created the design: the initials of our first names with our last name initial in the middle (like monograms on towels), the number "35" on top of the design, and underneath it the words, "Speak Love," which is the theme song from our wedding. (The song was really "Speak Low" from *One Touch of Venus*, circa 1964, but we changed it.)

My hubby, a basically conservative dentist, said that he wanted to have this tattoo in honor of our thirty-fifth anniversary. I thought this was so lovely! He is truly a Keeper. I guess my name on his arm means that he plans to keep *me*.

- Jean, Ann Arbor, Michigan

LOSER

Club Med Dread

My boyfriend and I had discussed going to New Mexico together on vacation. But then he announced he wanted to go to Club Med—alone.

His rationale was that he'd never done this when he was younger. Now at 36, he'd taken some time off from work to figure out what his next career move would be, and he wanted to do some exploring. I was dead-set against it. Club Med is for singles—the possibility of sex with a stranger is pretty much a given—and we were ostensibly a couple. Going, I told him, wasn't respectful of me.

He argued with me about how it was okay for him to go. He promised he wouldn't sleep with anyone else if he went. He said that he loved me now and would love me when he returned. I gave him an ultimatum: you go, I'm out.

We didn't discuss it after that. I thought he'd dropped the idea altogether, since we were still planning a New Mexico vacation. Then about two weeks later when I needed to book the trip, he told me he was going to Club Med after all.

I broke up with him that night.

- Shelly, Dallas, Texas

KEEPER

Afternoon Delight

Three months after we got married, Barry, a certified public accountant, had to go to Hawaii for two months to work on an audit project. I was able to visit him for a few days. He was working long hours trying to meet a deadline. Because he would be working, I'd have to find my own way to the hotel from the airport. That was fine with me. I understood.

But when I arrived, I started looking for the taxi stand. I saw Barry instead. He'd somehow managed to wrangle some precious time off. He was all spruced up and smelling particularly fine. He had a gorgeous fresh lei for me. Outside, a stretch limo was stocked with champagne, waiting for us. He had the driver take us on a little tour of the island. It was so romantic, a wonderful way to start my first visit to Hawaii. (Of course, the next day he had to work even longer hours to make up for "playing hooky.")

- Tracy, Seattle, Washington

LOSER

All Work . . . and No Play

Steve was a mechanic, very ambitious, and his goal was to make a lot money and retire early. So he was always at the shop—and he was always late for our dates. Not a few minutes late—hours late.

Once we actually celebrated New Year's Eve on the Garden State Parkway en route to a party because he picked me up at 11:30 PM that night. I was still crazy about him. I guess that's something you overlook when you're 21. But I knew he wasn't for me when I realized it wasn't just ambition. He was a workaholic.

We'd been dating about eight months when he took me to his parents' apartment for dinner so I could meet his family. He'd just introduced me to his mother when she said, "Your father's not home yet; he's still at work."

I realized it ran in the family. His father was a workaholic; he was a workaholic. I knew we had to break up. I wasn't going to be the wife of a man who was never home.

- Lindy, Manahawkin, New Jersey

The Good-bye Girl

My husband, Patrick, was raised in a family that doesn't like good-byes. They all tend to just disappear when it's time to go. I was raised in a big Italian family where we really made a big production out of every good-bye. When we were just married, I had an appointment to deliver the first book I wrote by myself to my publisher. This was an important editorial meeting and I was nervous about it. As I left, I saw him standing at the door waving a big white hanky at me, because he knew how much I needed him to send me off with good wishes. He doesn't even carry a handkerchief, so he had to actually go out and buy one. It meant a lot to me. I call my Irish, red-headed, blue-eyed husband my good luck Leprechaun.

- Nina, Houston, Texas

LOSER

Amtrak Gigolo

I'd spent the day in Washington, DC, and I was taking the train back to New York City. Near Philadelphia a handsome black guy—about nine years younger than me—sat down and started talking to me. Sean worked for Amtrak, riding up and down the East Coast, supervising the crews working on the tracks. He was a fairly interesting dude, entertaining and funny. I enjoyed his company. And by the time he got off in Philadelphia, I had this new friend and he had my phone number.

He started visiting me in New York City. Between visits we talked on the phone. The only frustration was that I couldn't always reach him because he was traveling.

Then he got a cell phone. That was wonderful. Even if his phone was off, I could leave messages and he could call me back. This was perfect for me. I do great when men don't live with me or in the same city, but when our time together is fun, romantic, and sexy.

One day I called him and left an affectionate message.

About twenty minutes later I got a call from a friend of mine, someone I've worked with for about twenty-five years. She said, "Shannon? Is that you?"

"Hey, Joyce! Howya doing?"

"This is so interesting," she said. "This guy I'm dating begged me to lend him my cell phone. When I finally got it back I found this really affectionate message, obviously not meant for me, in a very familiar voice."

Highly amused, we both immediately realized that Sean liked to pick up the same kind of women. Joyce and I are both well-educated, high-profile black professionals with roundish figures, light brown skin, and dyed light hair. We blew the whistle on him in separate calls.

I think of him as the Amtrack Gigolo. I wonder who he's seeing now . . . and if I know her!

- Shannon, New York, New York

Random Acts of Kindness

I have been married to Mitch for more than twenty-five years and didn't think he could surprise me anymore. But he did. For the Fourth of July holiday we were expecting company, and I gave him a long shopping list. When he came back he just dropped off all the groceries and said he had to go out for a little while. Well, about two hours later he came back with a big smile and a T-shirt from the local firehouse that had lost men on 9/11. He said he hoped I wasn't mad at him for deserting me, and then he explained why he was gone so long.

It seems that when Mitch was checking out at the grocery store, he noticed a bunch of firemen behind him buying supplies for dinner. Without really thinking about it, he told the cashier to put all of the firemen's groceries on *his* charge card. When the firemen realized what Mitch had done, they ran after him and insisted he stop in at the firehouse, which is just around the corner from us in downtown Manhattan. So Mitch briefly came home and then went to the firehouse where he was "forced" to have a little dinner and take home a T-shirt.

Mitch was just concerned that I would worry about him or be upset he wasn't helping set up the barbecue. I just hugged him and thanked *whoever* is in charge of such things that I have such a compassionate man.

- Wanda, New York, New York

About the Authors

Linda Lee Small is a writer specializing in family and women's issues. She is coauthor of seven books and the author of *Maybe Mother Did Know Best: Old-Fashioned Parenting the Modern Way*. Her articles have appeared in numerous publications, including *Parents*, *Women's Day*, *Redbook*, *Glamour*, *Ladies' Home Journal*, *Seventeen*, *Cosmopolitan*, and *Ms.*, where she was a contributing editor to the magazine. She lives in Brooklyn, New York, with her son.

Norine Dworkin is a writer and editor whose articles have appeared in *Family Circle*, *Ladies' Home Journal*, *Fitness*, *More*, *Good Housekeeping*, *Food & Wine*, *Natural Health*, *Unlimited*, *Las Vegas Life*, and the *Los Angeles Times*. She's the author of *The Funseeker's Guide to Las Vegas*. An expatriate New Yorker, she now lives in Las Vegas with her partner, Stewart.